A Mexican-American In Paris

Beastly Tales Romping Across

Pre-Covid Europe

The Writer's Cut!

Vol. 1

Jimmy The Pen

(aka The Beast)

Marquez

2021 LuLu Books/Jim Marquez

February 14, 2021

Published in the United States by Jim Marquez & Lulu.com

Library of Congress ISBN: 978-1-716-08575-8

Imprint: LuLu.com

First Edition. Non-Fiction.

Author: Jim Marquez

Title: A Mexican-American In Paris: Beastly Tales Romping Across Pre-Covid Europe! The Writer's Cut Vol. 1

Subject: Stories of Author's Life in Europe from September 2019-February 2020 & Beyond. Sex. Drinking/Bars. Adventure. Violence. Travel. Drama. Comedy. Coronavirus.

Book Design by Jimmy The Pen

For

Mom & Dad

The Great People of Paris/Munich/Berlin/Hamburg/Cologne/Salzburg/Vienna/Dublin/San Francisco/Pasadena

LuLu (not this book company, an actual woman; coincidence, huh?)

Gonzo (the man who allowed me to crash on his couch for 4 months as i wrote this)

Koreatown (Los Angeles) {i wrote this little book there}

To The Guy Who Stole My iPhone While I Sat At A Coffee Shop In K-Town One Night November 2020 And Then Gave It Back To Me After I Talked Him Out Of It

(amazing story for another time)

To the nearly 5000,000 (thus far as of february 2021) needlessly dead in the United States from the Coronavirus. Including my aunt and uncle and a handful of friends. There's only one sonofabitch responsible for this and I hope a new level of hell has been created just for him.

Some Words…

Hey, Kids. Your Uncle Jim here. Thank you ever so much for picking up a copy of this baby. A quicky, off the cuff, what the hell kinda project that I slapped together at the last minute in hopes of generating enough cash for rent, whiskey, and women. I hadn't planned on putting this out as a book but here it is. Like so much of the good shit in life, it comes when you're least begging God for it…

I wrote these pieces as part of a short series called "Yet Another Damn American in Paris". I was in dire need of financial rescue Fall 2020 and an old buddy of mine threw open the doors to his tiny apartment in Koreatown and allowed me to crash…turns out it was four months on that damn couch…thankfully…and while I was there I thought, fuck, man, might as well write something while I wait for my unemployment to come in.

I had submitted these pieces to a couple of major international magazines in hopes of they appearing at a *minimum* on their websites because I know how long they are. I knew that if they got accepted they'd chop out half of what I wrote but at least the check would have cleared. This was October 2020-December 2020. But not one word back. No rejection letters, not even a fuck-off stop bothering us. Ok, fine, been there before…January 2021 rolls around and I thought, fuck it, man, let's just turn this into a book. 'The Writer's Cut'. So, you get the whole cheese enchilada right at your fingertips.

Hence, with a self-imposed deadline, Valentine's Day, the furious re-editing of the work began, and, I added one more *cuento*, the Salzburg adventure, inspired by a long, lost love who bravely and sweetly restablished contact with me over the holidays and then just as quickly vanished, *yet once again* breaking my heart in the process. *HA!* When, oh when will this silly Beast ever learn? *Ohhhhhh that girl!* Oh well…in her words she's stuck in a marriage with a jealous, manipulative, controlling, overprotective man now who won't allow her to even check her social media…that's fucked up, and I am sorry, so is she, she agrees…hey, *I am* old enough to be her father, *I know*, but what the hell, the heart wants what the heart wants. Anyway…

I lived in Paris September 2019-February 2020. A life-long dream. Had been before on previous treks whilst a younger man, but not to this extent. While there this time I bounced around Europe but always came back to the city I considered my home. My original plan was to stay one to two years, *but then the goddamn fucking pandemic struck* and we Americans were sent packing. I did not want to come back to the states.

I was not ready to return to this violent, overpriced, overcrowded, traffic-fucked, inconvenient, corrupt, racist, filthy, entitled, paranoid, schizophrenic, shallow shithole that is my hometown of Los Angeles. A half century I've spent here and I thought that was plenty. Not married, no kids (that I know of), and the means to do so *at the time*, I jumped ship. In addition to becoming a welcomed local I lived through France's longest, ugliest unions strike, and I caught a near fatal case of an early variant of the Covid itself, which are discussed in the pages to follow. Got a little more than I wanted, but, at the same time, I got exactly what I needed.

Also wrote a book there, living in Hemingway's old neighborhood in the Mouffetard area, called ***"Among the Beasts: Coronavirus Edition Part Deux!"*** A book of stories about Los Angeles, oddly enough…I needed the distance, you see….for, as now, I'm finally writing about Europe while being held hostage here. That one is a great fucking book, containing some of my most dramatic, darkest, vengeful and loving work ever put-on page. People who've read it can't believe that I actually wrote something worth a damn. This one isn't as heavy or dark, admittedly, it's just a…well, it's a *romp*. Old word, yeah, yeah, look it up. And it makes me smile…So, if I were you, I'd get "Among the Beasts" as a companion to this puppy. Hope you like the both of them, and, again, thank you, thank you, thank you.

Proudly, this is my 17th self-published book since 2004. The first couple suck, don't bother, but from then on, oh boy! *Hop like a bunny!*

Dearest Reader, I cannot do this without you, and, if I may, if you still want, I'll continue to do so just for you.

Me love you long time.

Love & Whiskey,

Jimmy The Pen (aka The Beast) Marquez

Alrighty, then…it is 5:41pm. Thursday. February 4, 2021. I'm sitting outside on the patio of a Starbucks in East Pasadena. On Foothill Boulevard. The sun is going down. It's been bright and warm all day. They opened their outdoor dining today. I just moved back into Pasadena. What a contrast from Koreatown. So quiet. So clean. So fuckin' chill.

Coffee in hand… wishing my LuLu were here....thinking on Paris…thinking on her…

Contents

A Mexican-American In Paris
Beastly Tales Romping Across Pre-Covid Europe
The Writer's Cut!
Vol. 1

Yet Another Damn American In Paris

Craps. A whole lotta crap. Poo. Poo-Poo. Poop. Poops. *FECES!* Shit. As in *taking-a.* Or me being the Mexican kid and saying *Caca. I gotta go caca, momma!* (hell, for fun I *still* use that term. *Caca*. It's one of my favorite words/and or phrases. Like *panties*. Or, *wet-cunt*. I love 'em. (So, hey, what are some of your favorite words? Holy s*hit*, I digress). Or, when we're supposedly adults: *Bowel* Movements. *Oh my!* And then there's *fecal matter*. I like that one too. But that's not the same as the actual *piece of*, is it now?

No. We're talking about the act of dropping trou, slamming your fat ass down atop a wobbly toilet in a rank and stank hotel room somewhere in Paris (in a room much likened to the one Van Gogh immortalized in his canvas "Bedroom in Arles" but *here* I guess it could be on *Rue Monge* on the left bank: cramped, a tiny desk, hard mattress, can barely walk between the wall and the bed to the window, where, upon opening the double-door-French panels the boulevard is dramatically revealed to you in an explosive, late-September-day's-golden-hued-sunshine from the top floor you emphatically requested when you checked in and you suddenly realize *oh-my-fucking-christ* I'm in Paris), and then you unleash hell: a tornado-wide funnel opens from the end of your ducts in a direct route to your sizeable asshole and moist-noisy-splechy-*pounds* are orgasmically expunged from your wicked, despicable innards. ***Splash! Splash! Splash! Splash! Splaaaaaaaash!*** Into the bowl. The simple yet not so delicate sound of cement pouring from a newly replaced sprocket. That's how it sounds. *Oh, you crude bastard!* You actually lose weight!

Goddamn!

And because you are a conscientiously decent and good crapper you flush several times. *Not just once.* No. The First Flush is to be rid of the putridity. The booze you greedily gulped because you *willed* the bar to stay open until 7am. The hashish you inhaled that the bartenders shared with you. The overstuffed doner kebab you took in one bite thinking that might sober you up as you staggered south along the curving route of *Rue Mouffetard* toward your hovel, below, on *Monge*, having to make a hard left at the Starbucks on the corner down there. Also, that whore's cunny juice you more than happily swallowed with a bit of her blood for she was on the waning side of her monthly. Red wings anybody? Oh, yes, sweetheart, we'll always have Paris.

The bulk of that toxic stew is blissfully released.

The Second Flush is for the hard work put into the act of attempting to clean yourself. *You fuckling pig!* The mash-up of too much toilet paper. Dealing with the stench crawling up your nose and making you gag. Wiping off your dick-head from the pee that spurted out when you released anchor. That larger than you want to see dab of blackened-brown shit that sticks to your thumb and smears your palm. *Oh-fuck-me!* And more toilet paper because no matter how much you scoop out it's never enough. And you know the bowl is clogging up, pretty soon it won't flush and it'll get stuck. So, there's that second flush. And then more crap-paper after *that* to continue trawling for the dreaded *fecal matter* that you think you cleaned out but damn well know will dry and settle on the inside cracks close to the a-hole and stay there the rest of the day or night until you hose off with a shower attachment that gets up inside you real good; *oh, yes, son, sooooo fucking clean* that a barely legal female you bought drinks for at the local back in the *Mouffetard* can eat out your ass without any trepidation whatsoever. And then you flush a *third* time to finally be rid of all that Trumpian-pestilence.

Only thing is, on this particular trek to the porcelain altar, the *first* flush won‘t go.

Oh god.

And you’re due to check out of this quaint hotel in Paris in under an hour.

And you have a return reservation after you trek across Europe for a month, planning to stay again at this very hotel, where the people have come to know you, in order to continue your life in this City of Lights past the expiration date on your visa. *Fuck* leaving in 90 days! I’m staying forever!

So what the fuck am I going to do now? The clock is ticking.

It's too late to call for a plumber. So, I shave, brush my teeth. Turn, try the handle again and nothing. Stays put. *Fuck*. Ok. Shower up, be as ready to bolt as fast as possible. But first, flush again. Gurgling sounds at most. Brown and black water co-mingle with the floaters and spin around but goes nowhere.

Fuck!

They must have a plunger somewhere in this joint because what if something happens in the middle of the fucking night, right? If it's a simple clog a few angry thrusts outta do. Ok. Dressed. One last attempt. *Nothing!* A stink wafts about the room now. *Ewwww*. Dry heaving. Gag. Spit into the toilet. Mix it. Christ, I wanna throw up.

Fuck!

Hit the elevator located next to the room. Push the button. *Nothing*. Push the button again. Not working. *Fuck!* The stairwell is next to the elevator. I'm on the top floor. *Goddammit!* Around and around I go, as swift as a bowl of wretched, brown foulness should when a toilet is working proper. Not so bad. I'm headed *down*.

At the front desk there is a pretty French girl waiting to check in. I nod and smile at the desk clerk, a young woman I invited out for a drink a couple days ago and she had agreed but I had forgot about her and went out drinking on my own instead and ended up with a 21-year-old and her 18-year-old sister in the *Mouffetard* (not at the same time, mind you: one while the other was passed out and the other in the morning while the other was in the shower. The 18-year-old said to me, "Can I call you Daddy when I come?" I said, "Honey, you can call me Bugs-fucking-Bunny for all I care.")

Anyway, the clerk is saying to the newbie, in perfect English, "Check out is at 11am here, we have guests leaving now. At 1pm we can accommodate you if you can come back then."

The girl says, "That's fine. Can I leave my bag in your lock-up while I wait? I'll go to café. Have a coffee."

"Of course. *oh, Mr. Marquez, checking out already?"* she notices me waiting.

"Um…"

“Mr. Marquez is leaving early, perhaps we can make a quick turn-around and get you in his room before noon. Your luggage, Mr. Marquez? Would you like some help bringing down your things?”

“Well, I…”

“Oh, OK,” the young girl says, turns, smiles at me. “Perhaps Mr. Marquez can point out a few good cafés to me as he leaves. I’m from the north, this is my first holiday to Paris.”

“Sure, honey, I can…no, wait. What? No. I’m sorry, I can’t. I…”

“Is there a problem, Mr. Marquez,” the clerk says.

“Can I speak to you for a second?”

“Of course.”

To the side of the desk: “Is there a problem?”

“Well, um…the toilet seems to be a little stuck, I was wondering…”

“Yes, no problem, I will go up and take a look as soon as I check in this guest.”

"No, wait, hold on. I was hoping I can borrow a plunger? Do you have one in your maintenance closet by any chance? I'll take care…"

"Yes, we have several. I'll get one for you and be right up and …"

"No, please, I think I should do this myself. It's rather…"

"Oh, I see, well, ok, no problem. Wait here."

I step away, enter the common room with the free daily newspapers. I pick one up, headlines in French, and I know fuck-all in French, but I *can* make out the words "la greve" ('the strike'). A multi-unions strike was headed this way later in the fall, grumblings and rumors at this point (turned out to be hell on earth for over 40-fucking-days but that's another story). I could smell the sausages and eggs and toast and coffee in the buffet breakfast next door and hear the clinking of spoons and glasses and soft-spoken French between the older set, and the TV in the room is turned low to news reports of their Ex-President's funeral and suddenly I was *fuckin' starving* but had to shove that out of my mind and prepare my soul for had to be done in the next few minutes.

"Which do you need?" I hear the clerk say. She's holding three plungers. One small, almost backpack travel size. *Too* small. The fucker would drop below the water line and disappear into the muck. Not to mention my hands while using the thing. *Christ!* The next one, medium, about the size of a normal plunger you'd have in your bathroom. The third was abnormally large. As clunky and long and unwieldly as a Scottish claymore. With a claw-like suction cup. *Good lord!*

"The middle one will do." (I hope)

Handed over, try the elevator, still no use: *fuck*, the goddamn maids probably have their carts holding the doors. *Fuck*!

Take to the stairs. The first flight is fine. Second getting winded. Legs burning. I was staying on the third floor (French hotels are not that high), but their lobby is actually the first floor and so that means to get to the third floor you have to go up four flights of steps. I think. Or some bullshit like that. *Three floors, four floors, what the fuck does it matter?* I'm going to have a heart attack here. Spending days with my considerable brown ass in cafes, in *Ubers*, in bars, not a whole lot of exercise going on, yes?

Yes. Get to my floor, breathing hard (had no idea at this point I'd catch an early strain of the Coronavirus in late November and *then* I'd learn what *short-of-breath* is really all about) and the stench is palpable even before I enter the room.

Oh-Fuck-Me-Amadeus!

Throw the windows open. There's a strong breeze. It's autumn you know, and it really turns to autumn in Paris, unlike Los Angeles, my used-to-be-hometown, where's it's a hundred *fucking* degrees every *goddamn* day and there's fire in the hills for weeks on-end throughout September and into October.

Any-who…

I try to ignore the nightmare in the toilet, partially grounded from repeated attempts at flushing. The inside walls of the bowl and rim are stained with what looks to be maple-brown-sugar-Quaker-Oats-Oatmeal because the fucker almost overflowed but receded at the last possible second, *thank Christ*, and so now it's beady and flaky and crusting and wet and viscous and sludgy and toxic-wastey-like.

I shove the plunger into this morass of fecal madness, careful not to splash, and promptly snap the fucking thing in two. ***"WHAT-THE-FUCK-NO!"*** You hear the crack of cheap wood, my balance is off, my hands and arms crash into the toilet chasing the rubber-head-mouth and the wood attached to it.

Oh. My. God.

I quickly haul myself out. *Oh jesus it's all over me!* Not even a half second's exposure. Hands and arms up to my pits, my T-shirt, the chest area and onto my stomach, soaked in brown water and itty-bitty-brown bits. Ewww-*Fuck!*

I whip off my shirt, toss the fucker in the trash, and open the shower and bend inward and use the attachment to wash off my upper body, soap it, leave my jeans and boots on, try not to get them wet. Towel off. Look at the time: 20 minutes to check out. *Dammit.*

Grab fresh shirt from bag on bed. Try elevator. Not working. *FUCK!* Flail my way down the stairs to the lobby. Longer line at the desk. "Ah, Mr. Marquez, everything alright now?"

“Um, can I talk to you alone, please?”

Off to the side: I’m pouring sweat. “It broke.”

“The toilet?” Her eyes wide.

“No, the plunger. It broke in half my hands. I guess it was old.”

“Honestly, we have not had to use such tools in quite a while.”

“Lovely. So, hey, can I try out that monster plunger then? And I owe you money for the one I broke.”

“No, that is quite alright. Let me take care of this guest and I’ll go fetch the other one.”

“Great. Sorry. *Desole*. I am so embarrassed.”

“No, no, these things happen.”

But it *is* embarrassing. It’s one thing to crap so much or use too much paper and the shit, literally, gets stuck, but to break the goddamn plunger, to *cover* yourself in that shit? What a fucking idiot. And in front of the woman you wanted-*eventually*-to woo with cocktails over at *Harry’s Bar* and talk of world travel and literature and the whole time she’s looking at you thinking *you wretched-odiferous-fat-fucking-cloven-hooved-beast, what the fuck is wrong with you Americans? Must EVERYTHING be in Super-Size portions with you? And why haven't you ever learned to conserve your toilet paper once in a while? Why use a whole fuckin' roll when only a few pieces would do? Incredibly wasteful. Intestines drowning in corrupted bile. Dietary and digestive concerns a non-matter with your lot, huh? Just eat and drink and fuck indiscriminately and pray death looks the other as you turn and cough when you finally bother to go for a physical after 25-fucking-years. Yeah, good luck getting into my pants you fucking loser-you!*

Jesus, Honey, that's a bit harsh…

Drag my ass back upstairs. Huffing and puffing. I am drenched in sweat; hair matted; its overpriced gel rendered useless. I'm dizzy. No food yet. But how can you eat at a time like this? *Easy.* I'm already all cleaned out, remember? It sits and waits for me in the next room.

Ewww.

I flush again for the fuck of it. The black and brown and now *green and yellowish* water and the muck coalescing to it stir but nothing goes.

Dammit.

This sex toy I'm holding, this nearly five-foot-long dildo with silky-claw-end, is the biggest goddamn toilet plunger I have ever seen. I can stand instead of crouch and plant my legs for balance and I cram the fucker into its sickly, pussy-like maw.

Plunge deep into the pit of sin, yank up, keeping the wonder-stick and my hips at an angle and plunge again. Brown water splashes the upper rim, green water spills *over* the rim, it's still not going anywhere. Jam the fucker into the hole, shake, plunge, *wiggle* it back and forth, tiny pull-outs, teasing the hole, shoving it back in, *hard, hard, hard,* pull out, *"Come on you motherfucker!"* I cry and spit at the swirling merry-go-round of wafting ass-vomitus. *"Come, come, come, you impotent fuck, come!"*

The stench of it all is blinding as I jack-hammer the hole unmercifully. Monkey-splashing the water and all the aborted fetuses in the history of the world, apparently, onto the floor, the wall *up and behind* the toilet, onto my shirt again, my shoes, my jeans, *fuck it*, I don't care. This is personal. I've been here over a week and *nothing* bad happens. A whole wonderful-first-fucking-week on the trek of a lifetime beginning as smooth and sweet as a woman's drunken kiss, *and now suddenly this bullshit?* How did I anger the gods? *How hath I forsaken thee oh Lord?!*

Well, that's me. The shit always seems to find me.

And then, *what's that?* A gurgle? A belch? *A toilet fart?* I stop. Panting. Drenched in feces and whiskey-scented fear. I had pissed myself too. Wait. *Wait for it.* More belching. More farting. Yes, a distinct relief of gasses emanating from under the water, bubbles rising to the surface.

The water line, touching the rim, *shifts*, a wave that has crested, and begins to slowly, ever so indecipherably, roll back. Really? Or is that wishful thinking? No. *Look!* I think it's going down. Is it? *Yes! Yes! OH-THANK-GOD!*

Chugging quickly now, then, gagging, the toilet vibrating as it swallows, no let up, the worse thing it has ever been through in its up to this point dull life: assaulted; *beast*-handled; *bamboozled* into thinking this was going to be another honey dew slice of a French morning routine. For one second it halts its progress-*I gasp*, suck in barnyard-air-I think it's going to throw it back up, a volcano of sloppy chop suey exploding, spraying the ceiling…but the bowl belches again, farts, bubbles, and the remnants of another lost night in Paris continues its downward spiral.

I exhale.

Good-fucking-christ what a mess.

Oddly enough, I always make it a point to tidy up as I'm about to check-out of a room. It's true. And, *I know, I know* they have housekeeping for that. *But* I am a Mexican-American who was raised by a strict mother. Also a Mex-Am. And according to Mom: you never let them think you're a dirty-fucking-American (meaning *white*) who was reared without manners. Or, worse: *a dirty-fucking-Mexican*. That's the unforgivable sin, according to Mom. Don't give 'em an excuse to say *shit* about you behind your back. Have some decorum, she'd say. Have some goddamn self-respect, she'd say. Clean up after yourself, she'd say. We are a *clean* people.

Hey, well, yeah, different time…

So, I shower again. Clothes in the trash. Fuck it. I'll hit a thrift shop somewhere, re-supply. Except for the midnight-blue, extra soft Premium Levi's I got at their San Francisco store in Market Square. Pricey fuckers but the material and color have lasted. Not trashing those. Fuck that. Rinse out, stuff in a plastic bag and into my backpack. Hose off my boots and the now limp-for-life-extry-large-plunger-from-hell. Stow away in the shower. If it could smoke it'd probably be asking for a light. What was left of the first plunger, its rubber head and wood are a shattered memory. Trash the pieces.

Then, naked, I make the call. Talk to a different, older woman, she sounds Polish. Ask for towels and soap and large plastic trash bags and a mop they're never going to use again. "No, honey, believe me, be happy I'm doing this. Better me than you…Never mind what it is, just bring it upstairs. Knock and leave everything by the door."

I didn't care anymore. Get it done and clean and let me get the fuck out of here. Fuck, man. Time *to roll*, baby! Is what I was thinking, but in reality it's labor intensive, a horrid and pitiful task. Wallowing in your own filth may seem like a fun thing to do, but when you're over 40 it tends to lose its allure. Have you ever been on the tour of the Paris sewer system? (Yes, they actually have those) Well, like that...but on acid.

Holy-Mary-Mother-of-God.

A dystopian nightmare...slow, slow, slow motion, as if underwater, not being able to breathe...nothing makes sense...goop dripping off your fingers, flicking it off, splotches landing on the toilet tank...feet sloshing through the waste, crawling up your ankles, your legs, stretching and touching your balls and cock...dunking the mop into a tub of hot, soapy water, wringing the fucker out with your bare hands (forgot to ask for gloves)...scuttling along sullied walls...mashed-feces on the light switch, the sink, the fuckin' mirror for the love of god!...fighting, shaking, choking back the fresh vomit bubbling in your throat... the light is dimming, dying...the elevator next door coming to a halt: oh god she's here already!

She wants the room and the first thing she's going to want to do is take a crap. Oh god, not yet!...voices, muffled, it's getting darker, darker, darker...Your Majesty, the poor writers are storming the gates! FUCK THE WRITERS! Off With Their Heads! **Qu'ils mangent de la brioche!** *Oh yeah? And let them eat shit too...*

I shower for a third time. Put on my equally cool and super velvety black Levi's and a fresh shirt. Load my pockets: passport, wallet, silver, iPhone.

Down at the front desk it's now a young man I hand over the room key to and he mumbles *"Merci"* without looking up. *Ok, fuck you too! How much did I drop here again? And how much more am I going to spend when I get back in a few weeks? Fuck you, pal.*

But all I said was, "Thanks, man."

I had a train to catch. In the sitting room I ordered my *Uber* for the *Gare de l'East* station.

Outside in a steady drizzle the young girl who'd be taking over my room was smoking a cigarette. Leaning against the wall near the entrance to the hotel. She was barefoot, flats in hand, and wearing a tight skirt. Didn't notice that skirt before, but *oh so fetching and fuckable.*

She smiled. "So how was the room?"

I thought for a second: "Um…comfortable."

"That's good to hear."

"Yeah, hey, I gotta train to catch."

"Where you off to?" She batted her eyes, puffed her cigarette. *Mmmmm. Goddamn, I wish I can cum inside you.*

"Munich. For Octoberfest." (didn't know at the time it would be the last one because of the goddamn Covid)

"Wow! Sounds like fun."

"I hope so. It better be."

My *Uber* pulled up. *Jesus.* Fast fucker.

“Have a safe trip.”

“Yeah,”, I chuckled, tossing my gear into the back seat. “It’ll be a fun seven hours getting there.”

She laughed.

I waved, then, “Hold on,” I said. Took out my phone. “Real quick”. She struck a pose. I grabbed a photo. “Don’t worry, only for me, not gonna post it.”

“Better not.” She smiled wide, tossed her cigarette into the street, and went inside.

I never saw her again.

Goddammit!

Now, have you ever tried taking a crap in a public toilet at a sold-out Octoberfest in Munich in 28-degree weather? Freezing-fucking-rain and chunky mud all around? Well, let me tell you, son…

Salzburg, Wanna Get Back To Salzburg

I think on it as a dream…

A brief though wonderful wet dream but no actual sex took place for me there. It was an essence. A hazy, frosty, mid-autumnal magic that permeated the air, stroked my boozy sense of wonder, coddled my whiskey-scented soul, and, at the same time had a mid-winter kinda heaving *jive* to it. Dark so early. Silent. Breath pluming. Rain every goddamn day. Clear but mind-numbing icy at night. Tree leaves and flowers gone. Bars close by and plentiful. My only regret, and believe me, there have been tons of fucking regrets in this old drunkard's up-to-this-point-blessed and very goddamn lucky life, is that I didn't stay longer because I had such a hard-on to get to Vienna I had already rented an apartment there beforehand and so I was locked into *that* fucker and, thus, my shortened sojourn into the 'Burg.

Ok, my second regret was the room I had in town *here*. Behind a gas station with an entire street and parking lot attached to the hotel being torn up and under construction on a daily fucking basis. Should've researched that a bit more. Save me the early morning heart attacks of being awakened by pre-historic metal & gears monsters fighting over misbegotten territory or being *startled* awake by the blood curdling air raid type siren blasting like out of a muddled nightmare signaling the *end of days* from the *Salzach River* a mile away either because the rains had flooded over the banks or because somebody had fallen in and needed a fast-fucking rescue because that river flows like a motherfuckin' bat out of hell.

Oh, and no *Uber* service. *Bastards*. The only drawback: but fuck it, the inner town is so small that getting around on foot or grabbing an above-ground tram from the train station is not the toughest thing in the world to deal with. {Yes, I ended a sentence with a "preposition" so the fuck what?}

Late afternoon hangover, blurry, unsteady, *shaky* (as my buddy "joey" used to say), I managed to hit at least a few no-brainer touristy spots before stumbling off the beaten track, you have to, get it outta the way;

then, you can fuck around, pick at that pimple on the back of the neck of a city, pop the fucker, watch it spurt.

Mozart's childhood house? Check. Stroll the cobbled stoned lane he lived on? (which has become an unapologetic aberrant leper's scar on the face of the town because of said tourists' afterbirth). Check. See yonder lush green hillside the church where Mozart weekly played the organ as the boy wonder? Check. Get lost trying to find the entrance to their immaculately preserved 11th century castle (*Fortress Hohensalzburg*) they have on top of the mountain above the sales lot? Check. Lots of turns, twists, in a torrential rain, *higher, higher*, past pleasant enough hawkers and vendors under tents (hey, what's a little drowning-rat weather, right?) until you get to the way cool but disconcerting slanted-at-an-odd-angle elevator up the side of this treacherous perch and take in a (dare I say?) *breathtaking* view of the valley and river and rooftops below and then the town's church bells begin to ring at the precise moment in time you whip out your phone to snag a video........*fuggedaboutit!*

(See my Instagram, October 6, 2019, @thebeastlywriter)

Danke!

Or

Danke Schon, Baby!

Is that Austrian? Is that German? A 19-year-old girl drinking besides you in a bar will bite off your head if you have to ask. And if you tell her you just came out of Munich for *Octoberfest* she will say in nearly perfect English with just the slightest touch of a bunny-sweet accent, "Why did you bother? That is such a terrible place." And when you say you'll be shoving off to Vienna soon she says, again, in that huggable, kissable, oh so fuckable honey-dewed tinge of an accent, "Why do you bother? That is an even *worse* place!" I like Austrian girls. *"Now fuck the living Christ out of me, you big brown beast! I've never had a real man's cock in my tiny, tight cunt before! But eat my pussy first, I've never had that before either; well, you know, by somebody who actually knows how to eat pussy and make a girl cum! But be careful because I kinda squirt, I hope you don't mind! Oh, and I'm just getting over my period so there still might be a little bitty blood left. And you can come in me, of course, whatever, because we're of that generation where that doesn't mean as much as it did in an older generation's time, you know? Coming inside? That gesture, that act, means dick to us now. You won't be the first, you certainly won't be the last, and I will lie to my future husband about how many guys I let come in me because for some dumb reason I think, maybe, it still might mean something to a future spouse. That whole Virgin thing. They don't want to know about how much cum I've swallowed, how much meat I've had in my ass, how many guys I've peed on. I don't know. It's stupid. So, fill me up, go for it. Yeah, baby! But hurry because I wanna eat. I am soooooo fucking hungry!"* {sic}

Finding said bar is no easy task here (says I a year later, listening to the rain pour while also listening to the soundtrack to "Atomic Blonde" on Apple music, early February 2021, 'Koreatown', Mid-Wilshire Los Angeles, while sipping hot green tea, and having crashed the past four months on a buddy's couch), for most of these places don't seem to bear any precise addresses. Names above doorways on some, on lanes with the names, *maybe*, on signage, at the beginning of such lanes and you're forced to wander about until you think you've found the joint you're after.

{Whoa, wait: was that another preposition? Is that what you call a dangling modifier? I never figured that one out. Can I see hands by those who give a flying fuck?}

Too cold out to wait for the tram (not to mention the five freezing-wind-swept city blocks I'd have to expose myself to get to the station-stop), so I grab a taxi at the gas station outside my window. Give him the name of the bar, says he knows it, we're off.

I carry a short list in my wallet of, say, 3-6 *bars*. Prioritized by price (the cheaper the better) and by how late they close (nothing that shuts down by 11pm-midnight, but 2am, 3am, 4am, 5am and 6am closers only). Follow the closing times as you make your way across town. Want to keep the shit going, you know? Keep swimming, looking, darting here and there, a *beastly* shark, but, more importantly, how *near* these bars are to each other. How close are they to my room at the end of the night? Begin far out if I have to, then work my way in. Or, better yet, see if these boozers are located within easy *stumblement* of each other. The Irish pub here, the Spanish bar on the corner, the locals' boozer this way next to the kebab guy, the ex-pat hideout near the river at the end of the lane. Whatever, you get the idea.

Just a matter of past experience. I don't do one bar and stay the entire night. I bounce around. Though I won't travel 50 miles outside of city limits either because somebody makes a great this-or-that. *Fuck that noise.* I don't want to get fucked up and then have to wait for a morning bus back to town. Or wait for the morning train. Passed put on a platform's steel bench. Dog tired after 12 hours, *morgueshly* hungover, vomiting, pissed my pants, *crapped* my pants, *crying,* no cafes open, no food, no water. You feel like jumping into a river or stepping in front of the train itself. Unless you're lucky enough to have found a woman (which means less drinking because you're concentrating on the woman, making sure not to drink too much because then no hard cock for *anybody*) to take you back to her place, then, I don't want to be anywhere without quick and oft running transportation. I've done all that. It's an adventure and fun when you're in your 20s. *It truly is*. Sleeping in the bushes and waiting for the hostel or the "independent-backpackers" doors to re-open these days? Um, no. Not anymore. So if no woman, no more of anything to keep me happy or fed or satiated then, fine, get me the fuck outta there.

Get back to the room. Donkey piss. Strip naked. Climb into a king-sized bed, cozy and warm, empty bag on the floor of devoured mini-schnitzel sandwiches from the take-away down the street, bottle of water on the nightstand, phone charging, and pass out in comfort and blissful silence for the next 10 hours. And if the good lord has indeed blessed you-you wake up with the 22-year-old Columbian girl you met at that ex-pat bar, madly in love after having touched spirits for at least one night and/or morning. She half laying on your chest, not moving, not saying anything. Breathing shallow, a cat enjoying its early-afternoon nap. She *loves* cats. No hurry. It's like we've known each other for years…and I still love her. And I'm pretty damn sure she feels the same…

"What you want is in there," the old taxi driver idled at the foot of an alley and pointed to the right at a cobblestoned path that disappeared up and around a tall building that overlooked the river. We were sitting along the river on a one-way road. As were many other taxis for apparently a lot of other drunks come by here to drink. "The city does not allow taxis. Only the people walk, ok? Sorry. A little ways in, many bars, much food, is good." He smiled. (Insta 10/4/2019)

"All good then," I nodded, excited.

"Bars there hundreds of years old. You look up, see that everything is built into one of the mountainsides."

"Really? Cool. I'll be sure to look up. It's rare thing that people look up anymore." Hmm, somebody told me once a long time ago. I think it was another buddy of mine, Rick the Photographer, back in LA. "Ok, man, *danke*, brother."

"*Freilich. Bitte, bitte.*"

Shop fronts dollhouse-like with tiny benches out front, a curving cobblestoned lane, rising and rolling, a *Smurf-ian* village in this fairytale-like setting (my recall a bit cotton candy for I already had shots of Jager back at the room before I left, you know, to keep warm) and young couples and singles walked about with smiles on their faces, *lit*, red, *glowing*, happy, an early evening drunk in their eyes; that giddy-inebriation you feel at that age after having only a few and walking out of bars and directly into a pizzeria meters away, or the ubiquitous kebab joint, or a Mexican spot (the most crowded, and somewhere I will hit to grab a super burrito and have by the river to get a second wind and push on into the wee hours because I had a 5am Irish pub closer on my list) but here? Now? People quickly chowed down then danced into the next bar, literally *next door*, and I scurried into a Spanish Tapas with no tapas available only cocktails served up by young bow-tied Austrian boys behind the stick who spoke better Spanish than me.

American, huh? Yeah. Mexican-American, I say and set my phone down on the bar in front of me. Relaxed. On a bar stool *finally*. Not too many Americans around here, he comments. You want a tequila drink? Naw, something whiskey-based. You got it, pal. Then a young female voice: American you said? Yeah, you? Austrian, 100%, she gushes. And Gorgeous, I add. Your friend too, both of you so beautiful. Whaddya drinkin'? I offered. She called it, forgot what it was, may have been Sangria with Absinthe. Hey, boss, two more of whatever they're having. And a shot of Absinthe for me. Smiles all around. Really, for us? She blushed. They scooted closer to me. Why the fuck not? At the time I was flush with cash. And so, it's the idle chit chat. More booze. Laughing out loud. Moving closer she. A white-sweatered-no-bra breast casually rubs against my arm. A sly smile. The friend leaves for the toilet. I lean over and kiss this one on the lips. She reciprocates with tongue. I return it. Sly smile. Demure eyes. Legs rub underneath. I never kissed an American man before, she whispers. Honey, I say, neither have I. She laughs, smiles wide. One last kiss as the girlfriend comes back. Sits. She says, let us buy you a drink, what would you like? Whatever you're having, baby. Bartender comes up. Mind if I have shot with you, my friend? You're an OK-American! Sure, man, you buying? Of course. Shots of Jack lined up. They're buried. And another round of whatever these are; I wave an empty glass, the young lady is buying. Bartender nods. Leaves. Just out of curiosity and I probably should have asked before, but, how old are you, sweetie? 19. She's 18. God bless Austrian girls! I say. Cheers! And God bless American men! She says. *Clink. Clink. Clink.* OK, sorry, but we must go now. We have to meet friends at another bar. You are more than welcome to come with us. She puts her hand over mine. If it was just them two, yes, fuck yeah, but *I know* some of these "friends" will also include young men and goddammit I did not feel like having a pissing contest or competing for the girls' attention once those bulls came a snortin' around. Fuck that. Um, no, baby, that's nice to offer though, I take her hand and hold it. I'm gonna stay here for this last one then wander around, I say but I'm thinking *hanging out with a gaggle of teenagers isn't exactly what I had in mind tonight, anyway*. Our drinks come. The girls gulp theirs down in one shot. *Goddamn!* Well, we work at ___. It's a nice restaurant. In a hotel, on the roof, you can see all of Salzburg from there. It's so beautiful at night. We are servers. Give me your phone, I'll put in the address and my number. Come by, we'll buy you dinner. Have drinks after we finish. *Hell yes, baby!* But not tomorrow, she puts her hand on my shoulder. How about Wednesday? Perfect, I say. Gives me time to recover. Laughter and kisses on the cheeks, from the both of them, and tight pressing hugs, and, oh, wait, one photo, I say. Quick. Good, got it! Thank you girls, appreciate the invite. Of course, they say in sing-song unison. They leave. Bartender is back. And you did that how? I don't know, man, it happens sometimes. He chuckles. Ok, the girls are gone, how about something lethal now? By your leave, I nod my head. After, when I ask for the check he says, just gimme 20. Wow, thank you, brother. Hope your boss isn't looking. My friend, *I am* the boss…

Outside in the cold I'm staring at a ten-foot-tall wooden crucifix mounted 20 feet up on a stony wall above an alley. Tinfoil-ed burrito in hand. Head cloudy. *My God!* It's frightening and beautiful at the same time. Commit your sins inside then come out here to confess and pray right on the spot. Groveled. Penitent. *Doomed*. You were making out with a teenaged girl (legally an adult) at the bar, Brother Jim. Pull down your pants and masturbate in public. *Seek absolution*! Saith the Lord. *Huh? What?* Wow, these Austrians don't fuck around. {Extremely odd, is that I took a photo of this wooden Jesus, wrote a caption, and posted it on my Instagram, and shared on my Facebook, as I did with the other bits of Salzburg I encountered. But when I look back today, the photo is not there.

Same thing happened in Prague a thousand years ago. *The Baby Jesus of Prague*. Took a dozen shots and none of them came out except for one. His face was blurred…yeah, put that in your pipe and smoke it}

Anyway, the river: best place to catch your breath, take stock, count your cash, check your phone, snap off a few pics, grab a minute's video, *eat* for fuck's sake. This *Salzach*, in addition to running hard was a cold one, you could feel it emanating. Could see your breath after each bite. Much colder down here than in that alley hideaway. Look up into the dark mountainside above the town. Is that the castle you were at earlier? Oh yeah. And oh, look. More bars along *that* side of the river, facing the river, not hidden. But too far. Peaceful here, all you can hear is the stampeding water and the occasional taxi up near the bridge tearing out to deliver customers…

Was in a cramped cave-like bar before I set out for that Irish pub. It was indeed carved into the mountain side aways down from the tapas joint. Candle lit. Dean Martin music, softly. Sparsely populated. Half dozen old timer Austrians in suits and leather coats. Sitting alone. Spread out. A muted hand gesture brought over the only female, the bartender, maybe in her late 60s, with a refill. I sat at the bar and ordered in a too loud and slightly inebriated voice a Whiskey-Coke. Think it was 9 euros. All heads turned to watch me drink. Half snorting. Crooked smiles. Saliva drooled at the sight of me. *Fresh meat?* It felt like I was in a basement filled with serial killers. Here's what I wrote on a cocktail napkin and promptly shoved into my pocket: "Sorry about nothing and yet sad-eyed, little more than a middle-aged coven of paunchy drunkards'. Time to go. "On the house", the old woman said and put down another Whiskey-Coke in front of me as I was making to leave. What now? Well, I don't want to be rude…

Three drinks later

When the booze is settling in, when you know this is gonna get bad, but in a good way, *or not*, whoever knows?, it always seems like getting somewhere *else* takes for-fucking-ever. That food can only cut through so much. Beers mixed with whiskey and Absinthe and Sangria and touches of Jager and then a goblet of something lethal (whatever *the hell* that was) did the trick because you're floating now, giggling-haven't done that in a while-and eyebrows raised, you feel free, you know you're headed for the last bar of the night and you suddenly dart into a corner for a roaring bout of projectile vomiting and nobody sees you and nobody would care if they did and you find yourself agreeing with this, *grinning manically*, and one more hurl, *yes*, the poison is out; you feel fantastic, stomach and guts cleansed, nodding your noggin, playing "Sweetest Perfection" by Depeche Mode in your head as you round a corner, shuffle down a lonely lane and see at the end of the street people outside the very place you're looking for, smoking, laughing, glasses clinking, music that grows *louder* then *faaaaaades* as the doors open and close, wafting over figures in a fogging mist, outlines bubbling to life the closer you get. Yes, this is the place. It is after 3am. It's just getting started here.

"Personal Jesus" (off the same "Violator" album) is actually pounding as you enter and it is a circus. Drinkers. Drunkards. Imbibers. Proud Harlots. Roguish Knights. Compatriots in their late 20s. 30s. 40s. Into their 50s. Mostly Irish. Scottish. Welsh. Mexican? People are here to drink. Not kids who can't handle two shots of teq and a Corona. *Fuck no!* These are the *endurance* testers, right or wrong. How *long* can you go? Overstuffed tables, cramped booths, piled high at the bar, can barely make it to the fucking toilet. Of course pints of Guinness are poured, cans and bottles of everything else is available, along with copious amounts of both low and high-end whiskey from the Isle of Smiles. "DOUBLE KILBEGGAN ON THE ROCKS!" I shout at one of the men behind the stick. In jeans, a green T-shirt with the bar's logo. No foo-foo-*mixologists* with heads full of self-grandiose here, kids, these are fucking *bartenders.* *"ON THE ROCKS YOU SAY?"*

"Aye, lad!" I flash a smile.

"Oh, look at him, big man spends a minute in an Irish pub and he thinks he can speak the fookin' lingo!" People at the bar roar with laughter and pound their glasses.

"Aye!" I repeat.

"Ok, Mr. American fancy pants, name me one bar in Ireland that nobody knows about except for one of us. And *maybe* I'll think about serving you.

And *don't say* Fitzsimmons in the fookin' Temple Bar because every drunken cunt knows *that* one!"

For whatever reason there appears to be a huge population of Irish in Salzburg and, also, Vienna, I was to later find out. I have no fucking clue why. Maybe I should have asked because for my money, if you want to have a great time in a bar find an Irish one. Any city. Any country. No, not all of them are rip-snorting hoe-downs at a free whorehouse type, but if you ask, sniff around, you might be lucky and find one that fits just right… there's a lot to be said about getting off your fat, lazy ass and doing the necessary research. Especially on the road.

Anyway, it only takes me a second to come up with an answer because I had been there and loved the place and I slowly smile and say, "*Monroe's*. In Galway. Every Wednesday night they have the Trad. On Quai Street, I believe. Next to the water. They have some mighty fine *craic* there. Now, be a good cunt and go pour me my fucking whiskey already!" The bar top explodes, whooping and hollering, back slapping me.

The bartender slams his hand down and barks out laughing. "You *goddamn right,* Mr. American. *You goddamn right!* This one's on the house!"

Women bar side with their boyfriends turn to look at me. What kind of a cloven-hoof beast has penetrated their realm? Asserted their male dominance in an Irish pub where it matters the most and is now drinking for-fucking-free no less than five minutes upon entering said raucous establishment. Well, it's more like *leer* at me. *Ravish* with their eyes, perhaps? Some of them in long-term relationships are so desperate for something different. Something *other.* I get that sometimes, though nothing ever comes of it, but, man, *good god,* it's oh so very fucking nice, even for the briefest of moments, to be desired by women half my age, albeit through heavy-lidded whiskey-tinted gazes…

As for the rest of the patronage there seems to be an extra twinkle in their eyes and bounce in their step. Bodies herking and jerking, swaying in place. Breathing hard. Could be a blanket of cocaine has wrapped them up for the night. Keep the party going. Dunno. Don't ask. Don't care. Just keep my shit flowing, son!

"Mirror in the Bathroom" plays next and the crowd begins to jump up and down as a slightly older man walks up to the bartender behind the stick. "Who's this now?" he says and puts out a hand to me.

"Jim."

"Jimmy you say?"

"Yeah, ok, Jimmy."

"A good Irish name. Trustworthy. Solid. Old school."

"You're the boss, yes?"

"I am he."

"Great bar, man."

"Cheers, lad. Now what you drinking?"

"Well, I just got a Kilbeggan, but I can use…"

“Stop being a lazy bastard, get the man a drink now,” he slaps his bartender’s shoulder. “And get shots. All around, everybody here in front of me. *You bunch of cunts!”*

Another primitive pounding of the bar erupts.

“Now, Jimmy. When I say shots, what’s my man going to be pouring here? Jameson or Bushmills?

“Boss, come on, that’s too easy. You’re talking to an old man here. I’ve been.”

“Let’s hear it.”

“The Jamos, of course.” More back slapping.

“As far as I’m concerned a man can order whatever the fuck he bloody well pleases in my bar as long as his money is good. However, in this particular instance, the shots must be Jameson for reasons I know I don’t have to explain. But it certainly does my heart good that a fuckin’ yank knows exactly why as well. Also, I’m an old fucker too, and that should be sufficient enough explanation for most of the crap in our lives. Am I right, Jimmy? Can I get an amen?"

"A-fucking-men!"

Shots arrive, along with another Kilbeggan for me. They're slid along the bar top. We pick up. "Everybody raise your glasses. Come on. Get your drink," the boss says. "Raise 'em high, come on. *High* you fuckers!" We do. "Here's to you all for coming out tonight! And may you be in Heaven 30 minutes before the devil knows you're dead!"

"SLAINTE!" we shout in return and pound.

"CUNTS!" Boss shouts back after we turn over our glasses and slam them down.

"Just Got Lucky" by Jo Boxers comes up next and the crowd goes into a frenzy. It is deafening.

"Have to check on something, boys," Boss shouts. "Be right back." Boss slips into an office door behind the bar. I battle my way to the pisser. And after that…well…after that…good question…No, didn't pass out and come to in a Russian mafia run whorehouse chained to a bed with a drag queen up in the mountains (not that there's anything wrong with that, not my cup of tea, is all, but, hey, whatever). There may be an hour or so of this frivolity that has slipped from my consciousness into a special kind of darkness, that swirling ether of the bye-bye, a ball of cotton candy floating across your field of vision, a departing spirit, a hiccup in false time…On my phone I see a photo of me behind the bar and pouring pints of Guinness and the bartender and boss are on either side of me laughing…My arms around one of the girls who was looking at me earlier. The whites of her eyes are glowing and it looks like she is *slumped* in my arms…I'm on top of the bar with the boss and we're both shaking maracas in our hands, wearing Sombreros. There are crumpled Euro notes at our feet…Me sitting on the bar leading a toast with dozens gathered around…*Who took these?*...I see myself throwing up blood into the urinal in front of me, splattering pink on the flush handle and then creepy-crawling into the wall of the urinal and it takes its sweet motherfucking time reaching its destination. I flush rapidly several times to wash the fucker out …a young woman is jacking off her boyfriend under the table where they are seated with friends and clinking beers, his cock fully out, *sheathed* and *wet*, she's working it like a pro and as I pass the table the girl catches me watching and winks at me…I see a man is taking a swing at me, a long round-about type of swing, almost in slow motion and I duck the fucker and he flails and misses me and falls to the ground and his friends laugh at him and pour beer on his head and one of the women in his party kicks him in the balls and that produces a roar of uncontrollable laughter and the man on the ground coughs up vomit and fast crawls to the men's, having also shit his pants and his friends point at him as he slithers away, crying, his friends donkey-call harder…another table people are openly snorting a white powdery substance and calling for a tray of more shots…I pass the cloak room that is not being used for cloaks and see a man shoving his cock into a girl's cunt from behind, her jeans have been yanked down, the partition shutters at the counter are partially open and the man turns to look at me and winks and says, be a good lad, latch the shutters will ya? I do and as I walk away I hear, Cheers, man…and on and on, sticky filaments to unravel in that nowhere land of the booze…

Then……*Zang!*

You're back and it's 6am. *What the fuck?* Many have left suddenly. Or maybe not so sudden. Perhaps a slow trickle into the night. The music's volume is low. "Twilight Zone" by Golden Earring is playing. Boss is picking out a lucky few to stick around…You stay. *You* get the fuck out. You stay. You, Jimmy, you ain't going anywhere. Sit your ass back down. A handful of us. OK, Boss announces, one more hour, we'll go 'til 7 but that's it. Let's get some rounds going…I'll be back…He takes the hand of a young woman with dark hair who was standing by the side of the bar and looking at me with pouty, impaired eyes and he walks her into his office. *Dammit-to-Fuck Why can't I have her?!*

I think her name was Luisa. Flirty. Early-20s. She was sitting at a table and had kissed me on the lips earlier as I walked behind her to check on my coat on the hooks by the door. I had put my arm around her shoulders and leaned into her to smell her hair. We held hands for three heart beats…

When they came out of the office minutes later "Ghost Town" by The Specials was playing. Luisa was much more animated. She stayed behind the bar and poured shots. I couldn't take my eyes off her. She reminded me of a memory of someone I had left behind in the States.

Now, now, Jimmy, don't overstay your welcome, Boss said. I hadn't noticed he was quietly standing at my side. That there is my lass for the wee hours. Lulu, go wait in the car. She passes out the shots she poured as she comes from around the bar. We shoot. Boss hands her his keys. You know where it is, baby. There's blankets and hot chocolate in a thermos in the back seat. Lulu winks at me and disappears. Jimmy, let's go look for food and drink. My man will lock up. I know all the monsters around here. Get your coat.

Next thing I know we're hoofing it in the burning cold at 7:30am. Thank God the sun is still another hour from rising. The vampires can still roam. One place is two doors down. Boss knocks on the door. What are we doing out here, Boss? I say. Teeth chattering. Wait for it, Jimmy. A man, a server, opens wide with a tray and two shots on it. *What the fuck?* We kill them. Those were Blue Label Johnny Walker, Jimmy. Good, huh? Off we go now, next stop, Jimmy, Boss says. Keep it moving, stay warm. There are sheets of ice on public benches. The ground. Icicles forming on city lights. Watch your feet, Jimmy, Boss says. A quickened pace is made to a bar hidden in a deep cave built into the mountain whose entrance you cannot see from the road. *Bang, bang, bang* Boss goes on a monastery-like wooden door. *Open up you bastards!* Boss shouts. Bangs again. Another server appears at the door with a tray of shots. Ah, now *this* is what I'm talking about. Boss says. *Connemara.* A foul and deadly elixir that only the Irish can do so well. His nose twitches. This fucker is 135% proof. Bottoms up, Jimmy! *Ohhhhhh God. Jesus. It hurts. It actually fucking hurts*, I shout. {Yes, I've had it before, but that doesn't mean it gets any better} I know we could have done this at my place, Boss says. But this way we get fresh air, get the 'ol blood going, eh? Nothing like a brisk walk in the morning, eh, Jimmy? He was only wearing a sweater-vest over a white T-shirt. Frosty plumes of gasoline-enriched breath from the both of us belched out and obscured our faces. Lucky neither of us smoked…

When I was in Vienna, I went to another Irish bar on high rec. It's located on a side-side street, a dead-end, broken off from the main artery of a luxury shopping drag, a wickedly bland commercial tangle of lanes for the well-heeled to spend money on obscenely priced and garish crap, built for the local denizens and for those who view world travel as nothing more than a Nazi shopping spree on crack. And it was at this Irish pub, quite an amazing spot, really, décor-wise, and cheap, where some obnoxious drunk kept falling asleep on my shoulder at the bar and then waking up and asking if I could buy him a beer, and after telling him to fuck off for the fifth time he asked me how I came to find this particular hole in the wall because he's been coming here *for years* and has never seen an American, here, *ever*, so how is it that you…I mentioned the name of the joint back in Salzburg where I got the name of *this* place and he said, *Ohhhh*, you mean the bar where the boss is always, and he put a finger to his nose and tapped it.

Ha! 200 damn miles away and he has a reputation that proceeds him. I bought the old man a beer after all. Still was a dick…

A third bar Boss knocked upon, but nothing. A fourth. Nothing. Ok, fuck it, let's get back, Jimmy. We had basically done a loop up and around the cobbled-stone lane, once out onto the road that faces the river, then, fast-walked back to his place. His Mercedes was parked across the street from the pub. Which was already shuttered. After 8am now…Ah, look at that, Jimmy, Boss pointed to Luisa sleeping in the back seat under a green comforter. Sleeping like a baby. Isn't she beautiful? The most beautiful, I add. But I suspect there's much more to her than that. Yes, well, I'd drive you round to your hotel but, you know, got company and all. All good, man, I say, and shake his hand. Much thanks for the hospitality, Boss. Aye, lad, you're welcome, you're one of the good ones. Come back tomorrow, we'll do it again…Ohhhhhh God…..He then *slowwwwwwly* backs up and onto the sidewalk and hits a light pole. Then, puts it into DRIVE, and rolls off. You got it, man, I say and give him a thumbs up. Best of luck!

"Hey, I know you," I hear as I'm walking to what I'm hoping is a tram stop up the road from the pub in the general direction of back-home.

What-the-who-the-fuck?

"I'm staying at the same hotel, by the gas station," this kid tells me. Late 20s. Long, black leather coat. Knit cap. Gloves. Walking toward me. "I saw you checking in the other day. You have that big red bag, right?"

"Yeah."

"Well, you want to walk back together?" Think he's Canadian. "There's nobody out here to talk to."

I'm woozy. I'm starving. I'm dog-fucking-tired. I'm starting to crash. "Sure. What the hell? Better than standing in the cold for the tram."

We march down the middle of the road. "Keep in mind," I politely warn. "If you try to rob me I *will* push you into the river and keep walking."

"Don't gotta worry about me, man," the kid says.

"I'm serious," I say.

"We good…and I'm not looking for a sugar daddy either. I don't fuck dudes."

I laugh and I say, "Brother, neither do I."

It was a brisk walk back in the flickering twilight.

Our shadows arrived a little before we did.

Taxi In Hamburg: From The Personal Journals Of A Beastly Writer Called Jimmy The Pen

5:36pm....In room...*Hotel Furst Bismark*...Hamburg, Germany…Pouring rain today…30 degrees....listening to the best of "Joy Division" & "New Order" on Apple music, with the window open.

Day is shot...got up after 1pm (that's early for me these days running around Europa) and goddamn, I couldn't see the train station across the street it was raining so hard.....hung out in my room a couple hours to see if it would ease up; it did…went out for an hour...got bread, cheese, waters, juices, mini-apples, baby oranges, Oreos and eyeglasses, or “reading glasses”.

Past year been using the dreaded “readers” more and more. For reading and for the writing. Also, for the phone. But designer-like, with multi-color rims, blue or red, or pink, or green, very “arty” because, after all, *I Am* a fuckin’ artist, right? Ha!

My artist friends in L.A over the age of 40, either at gallery shows or private functions or boozing up at happy hours in local bars you have begun to see the readers: hanging off the fronts of shirts, sticking out of pockets, sitting on top of their heads…part of the costume now, an indispensable accessory…in addition to the flashy rings and extreme-dark sunglasses or obscenity-laced political rants on t-shirts or whatever else you see them wear that screams I AM AN ARTIST you see, in addition, the readers…*muy-goddamn-importante.*

I usually get my glasses at a $.99 Store, or whichever convenience-pharmacy-shop is nearby. The cheaper the better. I’ll lose or break those fuckers soon enough.

Anyway, desperately needed a new pair because I lost mine last night, I think, in the taxi I took at 4am. 4:30am. 5am? Don't remember.

Time, days, have gotten mixed up in my head.{It began in Paris for a week, then, I left on a 7-week self-tour across Europe before returning to Paris to live} Hopefully get back to the City of Lights for my birthday on the 16th, November…{mind you, this was the autumn/winter before the Covid fucked up our lives, and of course, stole a great goddamn deal of them too}

My first night in Hamburg, before I became familiar with the *Reeperbahn* district, was partially spent at a serviceable dive bar called "Mutter" because it seemed to be the only joint open on a late Tuesday night. An *early weeknight* for the love of god. Closer to the hotel than a couple others I researched but still far enough to necessitate transportation, especially after midnight. *Uber* is my lifeline. Call the fucker. Wait. Go. *Fuck* dealing with public transport. I want to get there *NOW!* It was bitterly cold out and I wasn't going to allow myself to freeze to death on a sidewalk waiting for the late bus…

Anyway, "Mutter": tiny, cheap, very much a locals' local. Patrons18-years-old to 50 years.. Music diverse w/DJ (various never-heard-of-music on CDs punched in with a slightly disabled hand by the lone bartender, a good man), a neighborhood brewer's beer on tap, forgot the name, and whiskey shots. *Everybody* smoking like goddamn trains. Convivial atmosphere though I didn't try to integrate as I usually do. No chatting up the bartender or flirting unabashedly with the waitress half my age, nor trying to take home that drunken, festering abscess of a woman at the end of the bar (whereupon at one point during the initial conversation before you walk her back to her place, because they usually live within walking distance, you'll hear the phrase "I'm bipolar, you know" uttered by said woman and you try to ignore that tiny, toxic detail for the only thing you actually care about at this precise moment in time is that you can still get hard after so much goddamn whiskey). *No!* This night I will shut the fuck up and just booze it.

After four-five drinks the natives assumed I knew what I was doing and simply ignored me. I mean, I was barely getting over the fuckin' gout that began back in Berlin Halloween weekend, I had to take it easy, you know? *You* ever had *the gout*? *Motherfucker the searing, crippling pain!* No lie. No hyperbole. *Goddamn!* Wouldn't wish it on my worst enemy.

And, so, nothing remarkable. No high drama as in other bars or places I've been the past couple months. No guns brandished. No fights. No raging beauty who wanted to take me home. No toilets overflowing. No army raids. Just blessedly *chill*. I have been to hundreds of bars in Europe and I specifically remember this one because of the fact that nothing happened. A comfortable and decent drunk.

Staggered out of *Mutter* 3am-ish. Place was still going. I was hungry. Had noticed a couple food joints open when the *Uber* brought me down the street earlier. Next block over. I went. Of course the bastards were closed. *FUCK!*...See figures fluttering out of the lights from up the way then darting off the main road and disappearing onto side-streets and alleyways. Look right, nobody. Look left. Nothing. No food. No other bars. *Mutter* the only life in the immediate vicinity.

Goddammit!

Ok, then, fuck it, man, let's go home.

Call an *Uber*: NO CARS AVAILABLE.

FUUUUUUCK!

You could see your breath pluming in front of your face, a cloven-hooved beastly breath, spinning smoky puffs of whiskey-scented cotton candy as you shuffle toward where you *think* the main boulevard is in order to flag down a stray taxi. There *has* to be one no matter how late, no matter if it's a mid-week. *Has to be.*

Wandering and discover a passageway. Long and partially lit. Graffiti splashed everywhere. The ceiling. The ground. The walls. Sprayed, scrawled, shat out, on top, on top, on top of each other. Layers upon layers, *years* of it.

Large, overstuffed steel waste bins bathe lazily in a lake of yellowish, milky urine. With such a stench settling in your nostrils. Good god. *Over a century of intoxicated-infectious piss!* Burns your nose. Burns your eyes. You squint. *Dry heave.* Rub your eyes out.

Piles of burnt clothes lay scattered about. Burnt cardboard. I think at the back of this thoroughfare was an open exit. Maybe a shortcut. *So fucking silent out here.* So incredibly-fucking-cold (how close are we to the North Sea?). No distant traffic as you might hear in some cities. A motor scooter. Train. Nothing. The only footsteps your own. Heartbeat too.

I step toward the passageway and stop. Consider marching on. *Christ this is nasty* but I'm curious as to what's on the other side. I push forward…and that's when a taxi came speeding down the street…

"GODDAMMIT STOP!" I shout, and drunkenly-an exceptional fat, old drunk btw-and attempt to take chase. ***"STOP GODDAMN YOU!"*** I'm in the street waving my arms above my head but he's gone. The street. The city. Abandoned. I am too.

And that's when I hear the horn. The slamming of brakes behind me. *Oh god I'm dead.* I brace for the impact and a sad, slow, agonizing death, *alone*, not having had any kids, a considerable bankroll sitting in my account {at the time, anyway, but now sleeping on a buddy's sofa for fuck's sake; *hey, thanks, trump!*} no woman, no bestselling book, dreams of becoming the modern-day Bukowski-Miller-Fitzgerald floating away as I go flying through the windshield and hurling into the lap of a sleepy but now startled Turkish man on his way home after a terrible night of business.

But no. Not to be. The taxi comes to a halt at the last possible moment. 10 yards behind me. I nearly pass out right then and there. Frozen in place. Eyes wide and unblinking. The weight of a cement block pulling my feet and legs into the ground. *God-fucking-dammit!*…The driver waves me over. *Laughing!* The window goes down an inch. It takes me a few seconds to break the paralysis and I waver up. “You need taxi, my friend?” he shouts.

“Fucking-A, yeah!” I say and nervous-giddy-giggle myself. The both of us relieved that a major international incident has been avoided. *“Yes, my friend, please, yes!”*

"Sit up front! We go! Sit up front!"

I do. Though I never like to sit up front, and that's where I guess my glasses fell out of my jacket pocket. It was cramped. He told me to put on the seat belt. All that fumbling and awkward positioning I’m assuming there they went…that sucked. I *loved* those fucking glasses....they were firetruck red.

I tell him which hotel. He nods. "So, where you from, my friend? England?" he asks as we speed forward and begin blowing through red lights and apocalyptic-like empty intersections of an icy city in the dead of night.

"England?" (a fuck-load of people think I’m from the U.K for some reason, no clue why, *got no fuckin’ Brit accent*. Nobody ever pegs me for American)

"No, no, sorry, my friend. American then?”

"Right."

"You here for business or fun?"

"Little of both."

"Ah, wise answer. How many days you stay?"

"What are you, man? The fuckin' *gestapo* or what?"

"No, no, it's I think that maybe because you man and you here for fun then maybe you like to go to where they have girls."

"Lemme guess, you get a kick-back for every drunk you roll into this whorehouse of yours in the middle of the night, right?"

"Completely legal here, my friend. 24 hours. Good girls. *Young* girls," he laughs. "And Clean. *Very clean*. Fresh. *So very fresh*."

"Fresh? That's doubtful."

"No, no, it's all legal here in Germany. I know you know this already. You look like man who knows things, I can see in your eyes. Unless maybe you no like girls...maybe boys? Fresh boys too. *Very young boys*. Good boys, they don't cry."

"*What the fuck did you say?!* And you know this *how?*"

"It is all good. *Legal* boys only. Of course. The bosses say."

"Who? The Russian mob?"

"I do not know of such things, but all legal in Germany. Anything goes. No shame."

"Dude, I love *women*, that's my problem, but not tonight."

"But to keep warm, eh? Is very cold night. You can pay for all night if you wish. A man needs to stay warm on these nights. Nice and fresh. The most *best* fresh. I promise!"

"It's after 4 in the fucking morning, I'm drunk, I'm sleepy, you think I can get it up for a woman right now? That's a waste of money. I can use that money for a steak and whiskey tomorrow."

"Ok, how about tomorrow then? I give you my number. You call me when you good again, I come, pick you up, no charge. because as you say, yes, they give me good tip for all mens I bring to the girls."

"Dude, I'm gonna have to pass for now, sounds interesting, but I'll get your number when we get to the hotel."

We drive in blessed but awkward silence for the next five minutes as it begins to rain again. Torrential.

Get to the hotel.

"Ok, my friend, that is 40 euros."

"40???!!!!!!" You miserable fuck.

"Hey, look, it is late, I bring you home ok, no problems for you, eh? All safe. All good. No other taxi this late you find."

"At most that should be 20, but whatever. *I am* home. Fuck it. Here..." I count out crumbled fivers and coins from my pocket. *Bastard.*

"Thank you my friend. You are good man. You call me tomorrow, ok? Goodnight. Bye-bye. Chow."

"Yeah, man, laters. *Danke, herr.*"

I get out. Slam the door. I never got his number.

Psychotic rain already easing up I go across the street to the train station. After 5am pretty sure. Sun won't be up for another three hours. Good. I hate getting back to the room in the daylight, but the station is coming alive. People waiting on platforms for local commuters to work. Backpackers headed god knows where. Many of the food stands opening. Grabbed a *hot* croissant with ham & scrambled egg. A *hot* chocolate croissant. A large cup of steaming *hot* coffee. A *frosty* bottle of Coke. Extra napkins. Bagged up then headed back to the room. *So hungry. So tired.*

(There's a drunk but subdued video on *Instagram* of myself taken in the hotel trying to find my room on this night. November 5th, 2019. @thebeastlywriter)

Halfway through my ham & egg croissant I pass out, face onto food and desk. Coffee spilt, raining off the desk and puddling onto the floor.

I do that a lot in Europe.

Papers, Please!
Cologne, Germany

Now, many know the bars in Berlin are legendary, but the bars in Cologne are damn fine too (Hamburgs' in the *Reeperbahn* district are *incredible as well…actually, truth be told, they're waaaaay fucking better than Cologne's*), especially right next to the Rhine River. Get tanked up, step outside, stumble a couple streets down and you're at water's edge.

It's a stunning sight after 3am: drunk, chowing down on a *doner kebab*, and watching the long boats, the transports, trudge up and down the swift-choppy river. Cold as fuck. Freezing beyond belief it feels like mid-winter but it's only mid-October. *Bone-fucking-ice!* And then it starts raining. Well, lucky you have on that $300 *Columbia* water-resistant-thermal-lined-coat you bought before you left the states--on sale, $80--for just this purpose. The fact that there *is* that river a minute's walk from the bars is what makes this area for the boozing extry special…

Anyway, you eat, you let the rain splash on your face. You shake it off. You hock up gobs of snot, maybe throw up, and guess what? Your second wind arrives because *this is Europe, baby!* There *is* going to be a late-night bar *somewhere*. There ain't no draconian-pussy-whipped laws here like they got in America. *They treat you like fucking children in the U.S, especially in Los Angeles.* Fuck that. You're a Beast, baby! You are *a writer*. You're a goddamned *Beastly* Writer! You demand strong drink.

--Yeah, I know, I was a lucky sumbitch to get to do all this the autumn/winter before the motherfuckin' Covid--

So, you walk back into the shit among the cloven-hooved-creatures of the night along cobble-stoned streets and dart across a plaza, dodging zombified drunks waving down their *Ubers* and snagging taxis. Turn right. Turn left. You hear music. You hear laughter. You've done this a million fucking times before, in many cities, many countries, too many to contemplate: faceless drunkards howling; unabashed madness, reeking of stale vomit and cheap whiskey and Russian cigarettes and frightened sex and the lot of them drowning in the tears of the manic depressive or the bipolar.

And sure enough, you find your prey. The doorman waves you in. It's packed. In these late-night bars you're likely to find a fuck-load of lost, middle-aged drunks like me as well as the young. They co-exist fine in these environs. So a man of my age blundering into a joint at 4am is nothing surprising to the door, the bar, or the patrons.

It's wonderfully loud. The music is 70s, 80s & 90s. Perfect. You make your way to the stick. Order up. Looking for pussy at this point is pretty much useless because you can't get your dick up after 9 hours of the booze. You want to scream, drink, flirt a bit, fondle titty, allow the pounding music into your soul, and drink *more* because you're actually happy for once and lucky to be here and alive and experiencing shit most small-town back homes will never experience themselves.

But this bar closes too. It's 5:00am. Still dark, still raining, still balls-freezing cold. You're within walking distance, kindof, to your room, and, as you resign yourself to that fate, you come across *another bar* still going strong. Not as loud or as packed as the one you left, but come on, *one more*. One drinky-poo then we can go home. *Maybe afterward stop at that McDonald's down the street from your room!* You can get a Sausage McMuffin to go. Hash browns. An OJ. And coffee. Oh god that sounds *soooooooo* fucking good right about now! *Fuck it, man!* Let's take a look. One more drink then we're gone, ok, Jimbo? *Just one-fucking-more!*

It's relaxed. Quite a few of the drunks are indeed older than me though there are at least a dozen half my age too.

A black woman in her late-60s immediately descends upon me as I hit the bar. "You looking for me, baby?" she says in broken English with a German accent. She leans into me and kisses me on the cheek and grabs my right hand. "I am not whore; I am not asking for money; maybe buy me whiskey. I want to make love. Come on, come with me. Take me home."

"Um, well, I…"

"I look like your mother, yes? You like your mommy? You want to *fuck* your mommy? Come with me."

What The Fuck?! God No! Fuck Off! Ohhhhhh You Crude Cunt!

Well, maybe *lose 30 years* and I would have, you know? Hey; the cock wants what the cock wants. I like 'em younger. 18-29. Can't help that. Besides, I wasn't looking for pussy, per se, as mentioned, *I just wanted whiskey!* She rubbed up against me, attaching a hot, dry clutching clam along my thigh and *grinded* but I ignored her and she pushed me away and waved her hands in my face in a *I give up* gesture and scurried off to chase down a much younger man than I who had also found his way into this soon-to-be unlucky den of inebriated inequity.

It was after 6am, I think. 6:30am? Finally getting my first drink here when the lights in the bar suddenly popped on. *WHAT THE FUCK?!* This is how they announce "last call"? By burning the corneas of their customers? *You savages!*

But it's not that.

I hear a pissed off voice screaming in German. A man's voice from behind me. I turn to see a wall of blue flashing lights covering the entrance-way, the front window; the door is open. You can see dozens of police cars haphazardly parked in the front of the bar.

Next thing that I should have noticed *first* but because I was drunk it took me a second is the muzzle end of an assault rifle pointed at my forehead. It is attached to the man screaming in German. He's wearing a dark blue uniform. Flak jacket with grenades attached. A helmet. Visor up. Gloves on. A balaclava covers his face except for *the green eyes*. They are wide. Sweating. Searching. Scared. He's continuing to holler at me. Off to the left a drunk at a table stands up too fast and another uniformed man uses his weapon as a baseball bat and swings it across the mid-section of this man in his 40s and drops him to the ground vomiting, splashing the wood floor violently. Blood comes out.

I'm nailed to the spot ripped out of my mind on bad whiskey. Where *can* I go? I've been up 23-fucking-hours. *What the fuck is happening?* Why is this man in a military-type uniform with grenades attached to his vest and a gun at my face yelling at me? *What the fuck?! Who are these people?* Are they police? Army? *Secret* police? There are dozens crowding into the bar. Spreading out and taking positions behind each of the drunks and pointing assault rifles at their heads. Men and rifles dripping wet from the rain.

But the only one saying anything is the man in front of me! And he is *angry* because it's obvious he's asking me questions and if I don't answer he's going to start blasting away. And once *he* goes off then everybody else here is going to get their heads blown off too. *What the fuck?!*

I can make out the words *"mach schnell!"* (*fast, or hurry up*) and *"schwine"* (*pig*) and I think the phrase *"wie heist du?"* (*what is your name*). But I'm drunk, I can't possibly begin a conversation, least not with *a fucking gun to my head!*

People turn to face the bar and put their hands up. I do the same. Now I feel the muzzle of the long gun pressed to the back of my head. *I'm shaking*. The man in uniform with the grenades attached to his vest is going off, still, *at me only*, and finally I say, out loud, really fuckin' pissed off and scared-shitless and in perfect-fucking-English, *"WHY ARE YOU YELLING AT ME, DUDE? WHAT THE HELL, MAN?!"*

It gets real quiet.

"Eh?" he says. Voice not as loud. "'Dude'"?

"Yeah," I say. "Dude."

"American?" he asks, perplexed. Immediately wondering what the fuck I'm doing here in the wee small hours of the morning, in this cancer ward, among these beasts, with a drink clutched in my raised, right hand.

I feel the entire bar looking me. Patrons. Uniforms. I turn to a half-lowered weapon. *"Papers!"* he says.

"Yeah, man." I reach into the left front pocket of my midnight-blue Levi's and *slowly* pull out my leather-passport case. Open it. Take out the passport. Hand it to him. (I always carry that little bastard on me because you never *ever* fuckin' know what kind of shit you're gonna get into. An American passport can be a lifesaver I've learned from being on the road, especially when you're a *brown* American who can easily be mistaken for something else from a cursory glance. Can't tell you how many times I've been stopped, questioned on the street, or pulled out of lines at airports only to be immediately dismissed once they see the blue cover and then open the fucker up).

He looks at it. Looks at me. Opens it. Sees. Looks at me again. "Hollywood?"

"Naw, man. Los Angeles." I take a sip of my drink and breathe because I know I'm going to get out of this. Don't know what the fuck is going to happen to the rest of my fellow degenerates or what prompted the local army-police to come storming in with assault rifles and grenades, but goddammit, I know I'm not part of *this* shit. And the man examining my passport may be thinking the same thing. So what gives? An actual raid happening here? Had I, in my silly, drunken state, found my way into an underground terrorist cell? Or some other equally illicit and nefarious state of affairs that would require the only solutions to the problem at hand to be those of the assault rifle and grenade variety?

He turns and waves over another uniform by the door, much younger, and with no rifle, not geared up. They speak in whispers but I clearly hear the word "American".

The kid runs out with my passport and hands it to an older man with no helmet or balaclava either and with white hair, he's waiting at the door with radio in hand. Obviously, the squad leader, or sergeant. He takes my passport and walks away. My ass clenches up. Thinking he might steal it or burn it he instead takes the driver's seat inside one of the blurry-blue-flashing light cars and I see the glow of a lap top screen light up his face.

He's running it. *Oh thank god!* I see him press my passport to the screen, as if scanning.

The man who was yelling at me has lowered his rifle, points it at the floor. His has not removed his finger from the trigger though. I take another sip of my drink. Lean against the bar. I paid 10 euros for this and I'm not going to let it go to waste. Fuck that. Army raid or not.

I look around to see a room full of bloated, terrified, red faces and raised assault rifles. I take another sip. Notice how now nobody wants to look me in the eye. Nobody wants me here. They know as an American I have a better than 50-50 chance of getting out alive *and they hate me for it.* They're jealous of that. At the same time they are also afraid of me. Just who the fuck do I think I am? To be here with them? This is *their* spot. *Fuck off, outsider!*

"Ok, American, time to go." It is the white-haired squad leader who ran my passport. He has roughly pushed aside the soldier who was yelling at me and had pointed an assault rifle at my head without the safety on and his finger on the trigger. He hands me back my passport.

"Ok?" I nod. My eyes on the door. It is clear of personal.

"Go." He waves me in the direction of the exit.

I step away from the bar with the whiskey.

He raises a hand to me. "*Bitte.* Leave glass."

I smile, try to add levity to the situation. "I just bought it, man."

He does not smile back. His hair is soaked. "Leave glass and go, American."

I nod, swig back the last of the whiskey and gently lay the glass on the bar.

"American, go now," he says softly.

Oh god.

Semi-drunk I manage to walk quickly and in a straight line while putting on my coat and make for the door without looking up. I am blinded by the blue, flashing lights and rain beating down as I breathe in fresh air and exhale a dragon's plume and it's instantly an ice box. My ears are filled with squawking radio chatter. There are army trucks with the back flap-doors un-fastened and ready to take prisoners. There is a command center to the right, away from the door. A tent is set up over a rickety, foldable desk and steaming cups of coffee and the older men huddled there, in rumpled uniforms, look at me and grumble and look away and I nearly trip over the cables laid out on the wet ground leading to a bank of lights that are illuminating the command center and---

WHAT THE FUCK DID I GET MYSELF INTO?!

I just wanted one more drink.

God-fucking-dammit!

It rains harder as I turn and make for my room. As I do so I take a last look behind me and see the soldiers swoop down on the drunks at the bar.

Rifle butts smack the backs of heads, people go down. Pockets are ripped out of pants. Wallets and ID cards take flight and scatter. Soldiers' voices holler. Chairs knock over. Glasses and bottles swept off the bar. I see the older lady who tried to get us out of there earlier shouting and spitting in the face of one of the soldiers, her hands and arms flying, and he ends her tirade with a bruising bash of his rifle against her mouth. Blood shoots out, splashes the soldier's face in front of her. He doesn't blink as she collapses. Slurred voices fueled by cheap alcohol raise higher, and then mayhem promptly ensues as the soldier's comrades see this as affirmation and too use their rifles in such a manner and the swinging and bringing down of rifles on *faces* and as well as heads and necks and prone bodies are initiated with gleeful brutality and wanton abandon. Every man takes to it. Every man and woman *take* it. No citizen review boards here, boyo. Their muffled screams still decipherable in the rain.

I turn away and vomit.

Crying, I finally get the fuck out of there.

I've said it a thousand times and I'll say it a thousand more because it's still damn good advice: *just get back to the motherfuckin' room.*

Walk fast. Head down.

Don't look at anybody.

Don't look at anything.

It's not any of your fucking business, son!

Check my watch: 7:25am. *Already?* It's still dark.

Good lord what the hell, man?

Make a left. Take a curving street, and I'm coming up along the backside of the Cologne Cathedral. Past the cathedral's courtyard, past the old church spire they have on display. Down another street. Past the liquor store and a souvenir shop that has been there since World Cup 2006. Cross the street. Make a right.

And ah, there she is. She's open. *The Golden Arches.* Lit up. Beckoning. Warm. My room is nearby. Less than 6 minutes-walk from there. People are going in and out despite the blinding rain, those sudden monsoons that pop up near the Rhine.

With shaky voice and hands I order.

I then sit.

And I take solace.

Paris NYE 2020: *Champs-Elysees*

I remember the cold. Always the fuckin' cold. Yes, I know, I bitch about the cold in a lot in my Euro pieces, but it's gotta be mentioned. As a kid growing up in sunny Los Angeles with 10 months warm and dry-as-fuck it was a mule's kick to the balls when Autumn rolled around during my time in Europe 2019, and then, into Winter 2020…

Now, for some dumb-fuck drunkard's reasoning I thought the *Eiffel Tower* would have fireworks at midnight for New Year's Eve. That thought wouldn't leave my mind. Even on the English version of *France 24* when they said, "Preparations are on the way for the only place in town where you can see fireworks on New year's Eve, and that, of course, is on the *Champs-Elysees*. We have {so-and-so} on site with details about new security measures."

I said, *what?* Naw, *fuck that*, man. How could they not have fireworks at the *Eiffel Tower*? Gee, I wonder if it's going to be cold sitting out on that grass. Wow, better take three bottles of wine to keep warm.

Dick.

I think It was December 29th when I realized, after an especially sober afternoon of checking *Google* for NYE gatherings in Paris that the only time they have the big fireworks at the *Eiffel Tower* is on *Bastille Day*. NOT NYE.

Hmm.

I guess I didn't want to accept the fact that in order to go there I'd have to fight my way onto and *off* the *Champs*, especially near the *Arc de Triomphe* where you had to be to see whatever the fuck there is to see properly. *No*. Fuck that. It's going to be a fucking nightmare. No fucking way. *Nope*. Not this asshole. Too much of a headache. Too dangerous with pickpockets. Police. Army. Crowds. Pushing. Street closures. *(I was here for World Cup 1998; I know how it can get)* Having to walk *miles* to find a designated entrance will be one of the worse cases of *motherfucker* there is. Because the fuckin' *Uber* ain't just gonna pull up to the McDonald's they got and let you out no big deal. *No. No. No*. Fuck that noise, no way you gonna catch me anywhere *near* that place. You need days of planning, a backpack full of booze, gotta consult maps, check for exits in case the shit goes down, and on top of *that* some kind of "super-flu" was laying siege on the city *arrondissement* by *arrondissement* AND because of the transportation strike **NO FUCKING METROS OR BUSES**. Yet they were *still* expecting 4-million people to jam that boulevard (there's only 2 million actually living here). From *the Arc* all the way down to *la Concorde* 2-fucking-kilometers. Fuck. That. Shit.

{And, in hindsight, talk about a 'super-spreader-event', huh?}

The clubs and restaurants were absolutely *out* too for NYE. You'd have to give your right kidney to get into any decent joint. Body parts or fuck-loads of cash. Either would do. Make reservations weeks in advance. Get on lists. "Dress-up". Um, no. So, a public event was in order. Brown bag my alcohol, go in my jeans and boots, walkabout, take in the scene, kick up a shit-storm at midnight, and meet a drunk woman: *happy new year, honey; come sit on your Jimmy's lap. Yeah, right there, baby, a scootch more to the right. Ah, there, oh my god. I love you so much!"*

My plan was to hit such a public event, then, about 2am, get to the local I had been haunting for months. Off the *Seine*, off *Saint-Michel,* within stumbling distance of *Notre-Dame.* The *Irish* pub (*not* the Canadian pub, and *not* the Scottish pub down-a-ways next bridge over on the left under that awning-thing that everybody has a hard-on for, nope not me, never cared for those two; *too fuckin' bright in that Scottish pub*). This *Ire* joint is popular with locals of all ilk. Black, White, French, Irish (*natch*). Spanish. French from the north. French from just outside the city. Ex-pats from other Euro countries who had *become* locals. I was welcomed quickly with open arms.

{The only American *living*, apparently, at the time in the whole of Paris. *No, just kidding*, but it damn well felt like it, and I didn't mind. I mean, every underground or local or club I was always the only American in sight. Sure, some Americans would pop up on the radar with their 3-night-stay-in-a-4-star-agency-deal then off for *a whole two days* in Amsterdam and then they just *had* to get back home because a neighbor was puppy-siting their new rescue; *christ,* those I tried to stay away from because whenever I told an American tourist I was living in Paris they'd get pissy & snotty about it, *try to dismiss the fact that I'm actually living in Paris*, that I'm boots-on-the-fuckin'-ground; *no*, they simply do not want to hear it, they ignore what you say about the city and try to impress me with boring speak of what little *they* know of the city. They tell of the lines they had to stand in to see whatever it is they thought they had to spend an entire fucking day in line for. And recite all the facts they learned behind whatever it is they thought they had to stand in line for. *Fuck off. I didn't ask*. And all the high-end shopping they did, which trendy restaurant they wasted money at, how much they spent on a watch (?) And then casually drop the name--like they went all the time--of the ONE bar they'd been to that tourists find on a safe-list of bars online for a *must visit* because they welcome Americans. Gimme a fuckin' break}

Anyway, this pub closes at 5am, then, there's the seemingly never-closing *Pub St. Michel* up the road after that (the kitchen always stayed open for me: club sandwich & fries). I'd buy shots of Jamos for the boys behind the stick. The kids working the door also loved their Uncle Jim.

I had a room in the *Left Bank* on the corner of *Rue des Ecoles & Rue du Cardinal Lemoine*, down the street from *le Sorbonne*, for that New Year's week. I sat at the end of my bed in my cute, knit 'beanie' cap (the one I'm wearing now as I write this), and nothing else, while masturbating and looking at *Instagram* photos of *The Perfect Russian Girl* who was one of my English students back in L.A. at the school I taught at before I was fired (not because of *her*). It was an ***ADULT*** school, ok? She was 20 years old. After I cried out the Russian girl's name and my heartbeat regulated I said aloud, *"Fuck it, man. Let's go to the Champs for New Year's Eve!"*

And so it began.

Four lousy miles from my hotel to the Arc. *Four*. But of course it seemed like for-fucking-ever. *Uber*, on a normal night, 20 minutes? Right up to that fucker too. But not NYE in Paris, baby. A whole 'nother monster.

So

Zig zagging through traffic along the river at a surprising clip the driver said, "My friend, you know they close the boulevard there. I will not be able to take you all the way in, but I will try to get you close. The rest you must walk."

"All good, buddy."

"'Buddy'. I like how you Americans say *buddy* or *pal* or I hear a lot of *amigo*, too."

"Yeah, we've managed to fuck up the entire English language."

"No, it's good."

"How about *Dude*?"

"Yeah, man, *The Dude.* We LOVE the Dude in Paris. We have a café in his honor here!"

(He wasn't lying about loving *the Dude*. I was able to check out *Le Dude* cafe in the *10th*, on my birthday night. It was ok: overpriced, overcrowded with kids ordering pints and after two they've had enough and it's time to go home early; *pussies*. The service was *meh*, but the décor was awesome. Very post-modern *Lebowski.* Check out my *Instagram* pics *@thebeastlywriter* November 16, 2019)

"We know English perfect here in the city, you know. "

"I noticed."

"Yes, the new generation watches *Netflix* and *Amazon Prime* and *Marvel* superhero movies and *Star Wars* and are social media whores; we also like to go to cinema and watch all the films in English. *Only* English. No problem."

"Yeah, I go to the *Gaumont* or *UGC*, the multi-screens, and all the movies are playing in V.O. and then there's maybe *one* screen showing a film French-dubbed or *in* French."

"Yes, for the older people, or for the parents."

"By where you picked me up, two doors down, they have *Le Grand Action*, and their films are in 70mm, all Hollywood movies. English only. Amazing. They've been showing *Once Upon a Time in Hollywood* for months now."

"We love the cinema here."

"Fuck yeah!"

"'Fuck yeah!'" he mimics and laughs out loud. He's maybe 23.

A few minutes of my head leaning against the window, thinking, *motherfucker, I'm in Paris for New Year's Eve*, you begin to see it. The ebb of a rising crest, inebriated humanity, on foot, in taxis, in cars, on bikes, in open-air rickshaws pulled by *electric* bicycles, scooters, the lot of them crawling, *purging* northbound, something on the brain, *a collective destination*; faces and clothes and bodies whooshing by as my *Uber* picks up speed: *my god we're making good time*! You can see boats in the river chugging along too, seeking the same truths as the others up on its banks, on the sidewalk adjacent to the road. Which is plentiful with bobbing balloons, stuffed animals, giant cocktails in 5-foot-long beaker glass tubes, topless women, dudes running bare-assed, frighteningly tall-garishly twisted party hats twirl above sweaty, throbbing heads, and the whole scene is accompanied by a wave of baby-push-strollers. Dancing, cavorting, ribbons in the air *and* hair, following an anonymous pied-fucking-piper to celebrate the coming of the third decade of the 21st century.

{*fuckin' 2020; aww hell*}

-----

45 harrowing traffic-infused minutes later we made it across a short span of bridge, in the direction of the *Champs*. Far off, but-keep-walking-and-eventually you'll-get-there-vicinity of the *Champs*.

Private tourist/party buses driving up on sidewalks, every fucking *Uber* and taxi in the city stopping at this one particular point of an intersection coming off this bridge and the sea of people marching along the river now amongst the traffic here, stopping traffic, horns and sirens blaring, police helicopters roaring low overhead with sweeping lights belting out admonishments in French while laughter and mangled voices, hordes of us, are involuntarily funneled through a canyon of cafes and high-end strip clubs with Bentleys parked out front, and shops boarded up and there were no other cars allowed this way, only the people, tens of thousands, *hundreds* of thousands, a million quite possibly from this direction, zombie-shuffling (reminded me of the two million of us storming the streets of downtown Seoul, South Korea to watch their match versus Poland on the big screens attached to the sides of high rise buildings back in ‘02), strays darting off to back street clubs, earnest doormen in black, ear pieces, pissed off, scared, nervous; if something happened, a gunshot, a bomb, there would be nothing they could do about it; the police would be useless, and the crowds would simply devour each other in futile yet furious attempts at blind, murderous escape.

A hundred-wide-body-wall of decaying human flesh being squeezed into one line for bag and body search is not a very nice place to be at any time in your life, but especially not here. Not within eyeshot of the *Champs-Elysees*. So close yet so far. *Fuck!* There are literally *millions* mulling about in front of you on the boulevard but you can’t quite get there. Not yet. I forget what the cut off time was when they stopped allowing people onto the *Champs* but I, and the many of those behind me crawling into my ass and hoping to Trojan Horse an entrance, sensed that that time was nigh.

So a concerted effort to push forward was in order. More so than what I had been doing. Slipping between bodies, raping the air, easy enough because of the material of my coat which was a raincoat type of thing and therefore slicker and *I slid* off the others, bulldozed my way, using my shoulders and arms to wiggle through, not stopping, *fuck niceties*. Even though the temp is in the 20s I'm starting to perspire. Breathing is bad. Air at a premium. *This is life-threatening.* I feel a pair of hands latch onto me from behind at a low level and assume it's a woman and keep tunneling. *Fuck you* if I was going to get caught out here. Being solo has its advantages. Don't have to worry about holding onto your girlfriend's hand, or wife, or a kid, or looking after your drunk buddy, or keeping groups of annoying friends together; just you, pal; only gotta worry about *numero-fucking-uno!*

And I decided not to take a bag either. No additional bag check for me. Just unzip my coat, they see if I'm *not* wearing a bulky vest with rip cords, and you're good to go.

Which is what basically happened. Everybody else had to dump their bottles of wine and champagne and beers into huge bins (then the complaining and bitching and collective sighs and moaning and this is the end of the end of the world as the French do), and they will now be at the mercy of the bars and cafes selling their booze at what would be fuck-a-stranger-in-the-ass-prices. What? $45 for Well-Whiskey & Coke? *$50?!* Thankfully I had the cash at the time but goddamn that's still an abortion of good taste. Motherfuckers.

I'll have two for sure, *maybe* three, tops; best to save the heavy drinking for the pub. Grateful to even have a place to go to later.

On the actual *Champs,* surprisingly, there is a calm. The madness to get here has dissipated and is over. *Good job*. Relax. Yes, turn and look south and you see millions, but it's chill, a reigned in mildly spirited banter, languages crisscrossing, people with their phones taking video and photos, and you look north and there's the *Arc* itself. Not as close as I wanted but I'm lucky to get in. It's 10:45pm. Perfect. Time for that booze.

The cold I was dreading--every-fucking-day in December it was getting ice-balls freezing--but here amongst the millions gathered, their body heat emanating, *seething*, alcohol plumed breathing, and the adrenaline generated, was enough to make it tolerable. You felt the ice in the air, but fuck it (for *now*). And quiet. You noticed how unbelievably damn quiet it was.

Most people who surrounded me on the street were tame. Standing or milling about, chatting amongst themselves, bored almost, nowhere to sit, meanwhile young families with children sat up high on dad's shoulders, all waiting, I'm assuming, for the countdown and the fireworks show. Wasn't exactly the raging atmosphere I anticipated. I thought debauchery: open fucking, cum shots spewing, mutual masturbation, titty flashing and free-for-all grabs, anal, ejaculations on face and/or tits, beat downs by cops, water cannons, chanting, singing, booze and blood flowing…no, wait, that's World Cup shit. *Dammit!* Oh well. I took my own photos.

Videos. The *Champs* lit so bright-white you could probably see it from space. I was here on Christmas Eve too, but the lights on the boulevard that night were red. *That* was some impressive shit, boy.

Anyway, couples and groups sat at reserved tables on the sidewalks under heat lamps. Couples and groups with no reservations stood in line on the sidewalks next to the tables hoping to get a table inside. Drunks like me stood in line not for a table but because I saw the bar deep inside the one place I decided to hover near selling cocktails-to-go in almost-quart-sized-containers. *That's* what I wanted. There. *That.*

But fuck the waiting.

The doorman was asking those in line "how many?" and when I said, "Just me" I was holding up a ten euro note. "The bar," I said. He nodded, waved me out of line. "To-go, ok? No hanging around," he said. "You want to come back see me."

"Thank you, brother," I said and we shook hands. (I did go back and true to his word I was quickly waved on with nothing more than a respectful nod)

Inside was chaos. Seven bartenders and they were *still* understaffed back there. Service for the tables outside, tables inside, and then us lined up. Waving cash. Ordering three to five cocktails per man. And yes, it was only men, unfortunately, crushing it at the bar. It took over 30 minutes to get a drink. It was a flurry of hands and dropped glasses went off like gunshots, and waiters slammed into you to get to the kitchen to fetch orders and managers cracked the whip. Phones rang incessantly. The doorman scolded people who were NOT customers to stay away from the toilets and chased them out--I took a monstrous racehorse piss myself. A DJ somewhere in the café was blasting away and people hollered for a table, cried out for drinks, demanded waiters. Overanxious humans wrestling with their primal state shoved into a confined space approaching batshit crazy, *and waiting*, just waiting for it to go off; for somebody to stand and heave a table through a window, to plunge a steak knife into somebody's heart, for the doorman to hurl bodies into the kitchen and onto the grill and for one of the bartenders to finally say *'fuck this"* and pour a bottle of whiskey over the bar itself and strike a motherfuckin' match! *Happy New Year Indeed!*

Outside with my drink I attempted to stroll, but again, *mellow*, the café was more exciting, and, you couldn't go far, too crowded, pretty much stuck in that area. I had the pisser and a bar in one spot close at hand and a friendly face at the door so fuck it.

It was near midnight.

Or was it midnight already? Did I miss the countdown? *Goddammit!*

I look up the street toward the *Arc* and the fireworks are going off. *Fuck me!* It's spectacular. Gotta admit. I love fireworks shows. This began with the music (hidden speakers along the boulevard) from a French favorite film, and mine, *"Amelie"*. A cooing sigh emanated from the millions gathered. Almost 20 years old that and that movie *still* pierces the heart. I filmed two minutes of this.

More music I forget what the fuck. I remember the *Amelie* because it was unexpected. That melancholic vibe to it. Caught people off guard. The rest of the show was disappointingly short. Yeah, big and loud as you'd expect any major, well produced fireworks endeavor but because it was exploding over the arches of the *Arc de Triomphe* I guess was the point.

Ok, fair enough. I've been in worse places on New Year's Eve, and, one *better*, actually. Las Vegas at the Millennium. *Year 2000, baby!* Anyway, the *ohhhhs* and *ahhhhhs* lasted *maybe* 10 minutes? Bastards.

And like that…like Moses saying this way, it's right here, just over the hill, *I swear to God*, people suddenly shifted gears, dropped every single bit of food and drink they had in their hands onto the ground (a startling contrast as to what Koreans do at public outdoor events) and about-faced *mach schnell!*

Oh fuck.

I'll wait. To hell with that. Grab another drink, take another monster piss and sit at a now empty table outside and watch the parade. Take more photos. But no. What took hours, hell, *an entire fucking day*, to build up, was now being released at the exact same motherfucking time. An entire population of a major world city heading in one direction: *out!* The stampede began, and I suddenly felt compelled to leave with them. Alrighty, then, see what's-what…

A third almost-quart-sized Whiskey & Coke in hand made my blind, pinball-like shuffle through tons of garbage and away from the *Champs* and onto unknown streets tolerable as I looked for a way back to the river. *Go south, Old Boy!* Go south!

Millions of others had the same idea for my fellow revelers too had their own bars to hit (I recognized names of such places bandied about), private parties to attend, carnality to explore and indulge in. Their voices grew louder away from the boulevard, more relieved, as if this were merely the obligatory family-friendly stop (and I guess for many it actually was) because the night was young and there was madness, wonderful madness to seek out. A hurried flourish of stomping feet added to the frivolity that was missing before: laughter, singing, bottles of wine appeared in hands and tossed into the streets, life had found its way.

And by the river as far as you can see honking cars, motorcycles, scooters, buses still stuck on sidewalks, walls of people rushed, drunk, alongside, between vehicles, a tangled morass of pandemonium and vomiting and men whipping out dicks to piss as children passed and pre-teen girls taking pictures of it and weed was in the air, *freezing fucking cold too*, and people drank from Jack Daniels bottles and tall cans of Boddington's and pills were being shoved into friends' mouths and that familiar French wail of police sirens permeated and pounded, providing a nerve-jangling soundtrack to a city on exodus for the next hours to come.

I don't know how long I dragged my ass down the street, river to my right, hoards practically running, I was fuckin' exhausted already. My pub was near *Notre-Dame*, how far can that be? *A-fucking-lot is how far*. My sense of direction was thrown off. Months in this town and I had no fucking clue where I was. *Just walking! Walking! Walking! Fuck!* But imagine trying to drive in this shit? Streets became parking lots *for miles*. Nobody going anywhere. After an hour this wasn't so much fun. Should've went straight to the goddamn pub before midnight and stayed there. Avoid all this bullshit.

And then there was more walking.

I could see across the river, on a corner by a church I think, a circle of motorized-bicycle rickshaws. No taxis. No *Ubers*. No public transport of any kind. So what the hell? Better than walking.

I dodge cars piling over one another across the bridge like ants on fire along with thousands of others on foot and make my approach.

"What do mean a hundred euros? That's fucking insane!"

The young, tall Polish man, rippling muscles through a tight, latex jersey with the cherried-out rickshaw (top canopy cover, safety belts, grab-bars on either side of a large, cushioned seat, a folded blanket on top of that) says, "My friend, you want to go to *Place Saint-Michel.* Very far. Much work."

"But a hundred? No way. I give you 50." I hold up a 50 euro note.

"90."

"60."

"85."

"70." I hold pull out a 20 spot and hold up both bills. "That's all I got."

“Ok, 70.”

I approach his rickshaw and hold out the money.

“No, no. You go with her.”

“What? Who?”

“Misha!” the young man demands over his shoulder.

Misha, downcast, walks up with bike and rickshaw in tow. ‘Eastern’ European girl. Early 20s. No make-up. Pale. No muscle tone. Maybe 90 pounds. In nothing more than a t-shirt, dirty, grey sweatpants, mud-spattered white shower sandals and black socks. *Hideous*. “She take you. She’s small but very strong. No problem. You give her money when you get there.”

No cover canopy. No safety belts. One loose side handle bar for the seat.

“She go very fast.”

“Great.”

“But no speak English.”

"Great."

I climb into a loose boxy seat, latch onto the one shaky handle bar on my right, and Misha pedals like a motherfucker to get us going. *We jettison!* Jump into traffic, careening off the backend of a mini-tour van, *jarring, fuck,* and cut in front of a delivery truck--horns shrieking, brakes hit, startled voices raised--and we immediately go into skidding mode, shuffling across rough gravel, the left rear wheel-chair-like-tire under my seat suddenly rising off the street then just as quickly crashing back. My balls shooting up into my throat.

"Watch it, honey!" I scream. She doesn't acknowledge. Continues to crank faster and we pick up more speed, which she expertly uses to weave in and out of cars that come close to hitting us but deftly outpaces them all. I hold on as hard as I can or I'll simply fly off the damn thing.

We get to an intersection of cars oozing off a bridge and attempting to merge onto the street we're on. Misha does not hesitate. Pushes forward, squeezing though the traffic, *barely fuckin' squeezing*, and we are being squashed--*oh my fucking god!*--you can feel the weight of the vehicles *pressing,* the drivers don't give a damn, raving-fucking-lunacy in their red rummy eyes; can clearly look into faces drenched in sweat despite the cold. Their windows down, cursing, shaking fists, spitting at us, throwing half empty beer cans at us, *at me*, yes, getting splashed and pummeled, so is Misha but she shakes it off, pedals *faster, faster*, grinding her bicycle motor, trying to get us out of danger of being compacted like junkyard scraps and for some reason "Cities in Dust" by Siouxsie & The Banshees starts playing in my stuffed-up head--those classic opening notes--and after we make it across this sea of metal we are promptly cock-blocked, pushed against the railing overlooking the river on a narrow footpath that runs *alongside* the river at the top of this bridge and we're trapped. Within seconds a half dozen other rickshaws join us amidst their own deranged chorus of shrieking car horns and bellowed curses and projectile food scraps. Her workmates, startled, flustered, maddened, and others attempting this shit tonight to make quick money and no doubt having regretted doing so start yammering at each other, pissed at the traffic, gesturing at their rigs, pointing wildly, assuming they're figuring out another route to get wherever the hell they're supposed to be going and I can't see their customers' faces because their backseats have canopies over their heads and are keeping warmer than I am, *gotta be*, because my fucking fingers are fusing with the steel stripper pole I'm clinging onto to stay alive.

One driver, a man, begins to wave the others to follow him, he apparently knows a way out of this mess and turns his rig against the flow of traffic and heads back over the bridge and Misha looks over her shoulder at me and with her thin arms hugs herself and I'm guessing she's telling me to hold on because she aims her bike after the others and we take flight.

{"Under Pressure" By Queen & Bowie is the next tune in my frozen, drunk head that begins to play}

I take out my phone, secure it in the folds of my coat's zipper (wearing it like a cop's body cam) and press video to record the following…

Misha cranks the pedals only once and gravity does the rest. It's a neck-snapping jolt of speed and this path is way fucking steeper than I thought it was and I lean back into my bucket seat, use *both* hands to hold on and the wind kicks up and…*awwwww, fuck! Watchit!*

A food delivery motor scooter jumps the curb and makes haste head-on into Misha's right-away. *Those delivery fuckers have no soul*, and this pick-up game of "chicken" ends as fast as it started for Misha has to snap her bike to the right to avoid the collision and slams into the railing overlooking the River Seine and my end of the rig fishtails, bounces off the metal railing and I'm jerked sideways and I remember seeing my left hand in slow motion reaching out for one of the rusted horizontal pipes in front of me that makes up the safety barrier and I latch onto *that* and my right hand hangs onto the seat-pole but my body continues toward the river and I hear Misha scream but goddamn luckily the railing is air tight (*thank you French engineering*) and it catches me by my drunkard's paunch and I'm promptly thrown back onto my seat.

Owww-Motherfucker! Rubbing my mid-section.

I can't swim. And. Because of the temperature and rapid flow, if I hadn't drowned within the first few seconds, I certainly would have frozen to death and nobody would've known nor given a damn but poor Misha there. Also, because I'm a klutz, I probably would have landed bad, broken my neck, and be dead even before I entered the water. Either way. *Fucked.*

I hear, "Ok? Ok?" It's Misha. "Ok?" She's hollering, in panic because she almost lost a passenger to the river and *may* be fired, or because time is wasting. Obviously I'm still amongst the beasts so she begins to pedal in place to get the motor started and I shout back, waving my hand at her, *"Go! Go! Go!"*

She does. No time to fret. Time is money. *No Money (t). No honey.* The faster she gets my fat ass to the pub the faster she can get back onto the road. I get it. Fine. But *goddamn*, you know?

I swat at my chest to see if my phone is still there. Yep. And I got it all on video!

Fuck yeah!

And I swat at my chest again to get my heart started.

Rolling downhill we must be doing a bumpy 30mph. Screams of terror and exhilaration from both driver and passenger alike only a few ticks ahead of us. My arms and legs flailing, Misha trying to keep us upright, the force of 250 drunk-Mexican-pounds pushing at her back at speed is almost too much. She's gonna crack in half.

Other drivers are laughing like loons, digging it because they've got a way out of dodge now. We make a wide turn, the gaggle of us, coming off the bridge and again my rear tire rises but comes back down onto a cobblestone street.

Soooooooo quiet suddenly. *Spooky. Like traipsing through an old Scottish graveyard Scooby-fucking-Doo kinda spooky.* There's nobody here. The traffic and revelers have disappeared. Only us. You can hear the tires whisper-rolling over the ground. Hear the lawnmower-like whine of the motors gurgling. *What street are we on?* Is that the Ferris wheel? *This is incredible.* A private tour on the streets of Paris. *Blistering-fucking-cold* though, and a breeze has kicked up to make it worse but this, believe it or not, is the most comfortable I've been all night.

In my head "The Killing Moon" by Echo & The Buunymen begins to play as we silently wheel pass the *Palais-Royal* after 3am-ish…as ghosts we skirt pass the *Louvre…*..did we just come off the *Rue de Rivoli?* Yes. Well, fuck me. And there's nobody anywhere!

Enjoying the hell out of this we cross another bridge as my fellow travellers scatter into the night and you can see *Notre-Dame.* Oh thank god…(funny, when I first arrived in Paris I was excited as a school boy who just fingered his first cunny to see all these monuments, though I had seen before on shorter treks, *but living here now*, *wow*; chugging past, in *Ubers*, taxis, trains; after the hundredth time blowing by the *Eiffel Tower* or *Notre-Dame* you don't give them a second glance, it becomes another part of the landscape as you're getting your shit done).

Teeth chat-chat-chattering……body shaking…back killing me….OK, enough. I can walk to the pub from here. *Wait.* No. Check that. I don't think I have legs or an ass anymore. Better let Misha finish this. We skip over the *Ile de La Cite* and then right onto *Quai de Grandes Augustins* (oh fuck, I see Pub St. Michel is closed tonight, *that sucks*, hoping to get food there later, but the corner café is open and overflowing with newly arrived revelers though no real bar inside to speak of), clear the gigantic intersection of *Saint-Michel,* and pull over. Across the road from the Irish Pub, alongside the river once again. Done and done. *Finally.*

Misha is panting, shivering, lips and face blue, drenched in beer and wine. One of her filthy shower sandals is missing. I nearly fall out of the boxy seat, my legs and arms cramped, unfolding, shaky. *Jesus-fucking-Christ!*

I hand her the 70 euros. I say, "How much does the boss get?" she says in broken English, "50." I shake my head and mumble "*asshole*". I take out another 20. "Fuck him. Here's some extra for you. You keep, huh?" She half smiles, nods, tucks it in to her waist band. Then, hops onto her bike and jettisons off. Back into the shit…

"The Politics of Dancing" by Re-Flex is blasting as I enter the pub. It's packed. There was a line to get in at 4am but the doorman knows me. We hug, wish each other 'happy new year' in French. The female bartenders are dancing behind the stick, cackling with delight, happy as hell, and it's infectious. *Thank you, ladies!* I gently force my way to the bar and order shots for everybody working it. Still somewhat shaky.

One of the dude-tenders shakes my hand, we can barely hear each other as he also pours me a shot of *Jamos. Oh goddamn.* Never needed a drink so fucking bad. He pours his. We cheers. Pours me another. I reach for my wallet, he waves me off, hollers, *"Your money's no good here tonight!"* Goddamn it's so good to be The Beast, and also in a foreign land, apparently.

I put my iPhone on the bar top in front of me at my favorite seat as I always do. Lean against the bar, not sitting. Skim the past couple hours of my life. The freakish traffic. My almost-spill into the river. The hushed back streets. Not to mention the crowds and fireworks over at the *Champs.* I am one lucky sonofabitch. Can't wait to post this shit.

"Jim!" I hear my name called. *"JIM!"*

What the fuck?

From a corner table by the window a French girl. 25 years old. So pretty. I know her. Met her a few times before at other bars after midnight. Or 5am. Later once or twice. Bit of a sweet drunk (hey, who isn't around here?) and a little depressed with a tiny dash of low self-esteem. *I loved her.* From a small town outside the city. A server at a café, nearby, somewhere.

She waves me over. I'm tired. Fuck that. I wave *her* over. She was sitting with a young gay couple who were cuddling and probably felt left out for she just about jumps out of her seat and, the waitress she is, negotiates the crush of people stumbling into each other, spilling booze, dropping shit, and is at my side, snuggling up to me. Her wet-denim crotch clamping onto my left leg. We kiss on each cheek, then, she pecks me on the lips. She's had a few already, *dammit*; I'm completely sober at this point thanks to *Mr. Toad's Wild Ride* out there and the bitter fucking cold, and she says, *"Oh my god, Jimmy! I was looking for you!"*

"You were?"

"Yes, remember you said last time we should meet for New Year's Eve here?"

Bullshit. I never said that. "Oh, right, yeah!" I say. "Come here, baby!" I kiss her fully on the lips and press an out-of-nowhere, *fast*, erection against her.

She allows that and says, *"Buy me a Whiskey-Coke, Jimmy. Then we go sit at my table and talk."*

I turn and my buddy is setting us up. He says, smiling wide, "She actually was asking for you earlier." Winks. Pours extra shots for he and me and we shoot. Nice.

I turn to hand her-her drink. I use my left arm to bring us together again. I'm standing at an odd angle, facing her and the bar. We wish Happy New Year. We kiss like lovers. "Atomic" by Blondie comes on and we embrace and---

--I'm shoved into my girl and I reach out a hand to brace us from hitting the bar but we *slam* against the bar, anyway, though not as hard as we would have, and my drink goes flying across the bar top. Her drink crashes to the floor as I'm shoved again and I go half way to my knees, my girl trying to hold me up and somebody kicks me in the ribs and knocks me back against the base of the counter and I see a flash of an arm in white as I glance up, wincing, *a hoodie*, maybe, and the fucker snatches my phone off the bar and pushes his way into the crowd hightailing it, making for the door. People around us laugh, they didn't see what happened, somebody shouts, *"Hey you two no rough sex here!"* and I scream out *"**MOTHERFUCKER!**"* My girl pulls me up, hugs me, crying, and the female manager of the pub leans over the bar and grabs my shoulder from behind and says, *"You ok, Jimmy? What happened?"*

"That motherfucker assaulted me and stole my phone! *Right here, right now!"*

She doesn't hesitate. She swings her legs over the bar, hops off and starts running. *"WHITE HOODIE!"* I yell after her.

She gets to the door, grabs the doorman, and I see them fly past the front window in chase.

"You ok, baby?" I say to my girl.

"Yes, yes, just startled." Wiping tears. "You hurt?"

"No…in shock is all…"

"Come, let's sit, and wait."

"Fuck!" I scream. *"My fucking phone!"*

"I know." She rubs at the side of my head. "I know, baby. *Shhhh.*" She's taken my arm and is leading me back to her table. Her friends have left. "You're lucky he didn't have a knife," she offers. And I smile, thinking, yeah, only in Europe can you possibly say that, huh? Back in L.A. the motherfuckin'-mutt would have shot me in the head for it. Because that's Los Angeles.

"My whole life here since September was on that phone." I say and I let her seat me. "All the pictures and notes and maps and schedules and research and videos. *Oh my god all my videos!*" I see the shit I went through to get here tonight……*Vanished*……I didn't have time to edit or post any of it……*Gone with everything else*……My life in Europe only to be recalled in long-winded stories. Writing whilst sitting on the sofa I current sleep on at a friend's apartment, broke, waiting for government assistance as the fucking Covid runs rampant through the streets of L.A. late December 2020.

God-Fucking-Dammit!

"You have insurance yes?"

"Yes."

"That is good then. You go to Apple store and get a new one."

"The one Apple store in this town you have to make an appointment to visit two weeks in advance you mean?"

"*Shhhh*. Relax. I will get us more drinks. Calm down. I'll give you a few minutes." She kisses me on the lips and dashes off.

Fuck! Goddammit! Fuck!

I'm left to stew. Muttering under my breath. Angry. Scared. *What the hell, man?!* Lower my head. Rub at my side. Not too bad. I was robbed once before and had the shit beaten out of me back in Downtown LA about seven years ago. Two drug dealing cowards from behind, with a hunting knife and a gun. *That* was a beating. Well-deserved. Well taken.

But I'm still shaking my head. Cursing myself for being so goddamn stupid as to simply leave my phone on the bar. *But why not?* I know half the people in the joint. I was standing right above it. Why worry I'd get robbed *here* of all places? Maybe I was acting too beastly for some lonely, self-loathing-fuck-face-loser-son-of-a-bitch to handle. And with a hot French girl half my age at that.

Fuck him.

I hope he drowns in the river. I hope somebody slices his throat and tosses him *into* the river. Gets washed out to sea. I mean, why bother? I have face ID on that thing *and* a passcode. He can't possibly get in. Fuckin' moron.

"We get our phones from the *Orange* shop. They have pay-as-you-go smartphones." My girl says upon returning with *pint-sized* glasses of Whiskey & Coke. "If you need to we can go together after the holiday. They have a location over here on *Michel.*" She kisses me on the cheek. "Besides, you have automatic save in the cloud, yes? For when you get your replacement." *Oh, yeah, riiiiiight!* "Drink, baby." I do.

(*Orange*. Not the best, but it did the trick. You pay for 20 days or whatever at a time. It would be over two months until I got a replacement. Couldn't do it in Paris. It was a major fuckin' bitch to get done. Over two-hundred-goddamn dollars too. Talk about getting fucked in the ass by a stranger. When I received the phone at my hotel in San Francisco I nearly fainted to see that yup, everything indeed was 'in the cloud' EXCEPT for NYE Paris. *What The Fuck?! NOOOOOOO! HOW IS THAT POSSIBLE IF EVERYTHING ELSE DURING THE DAMN DAY ON THE 31st IS THERE?! NOT FAIR!)*

My girl leans against my shoulder. Just then the manager comes back, spots me right away. Holds her hands up. Empty. "Sorry, man. He got away. You want me to call the police, make a report?" It's after 5am on NYE. Who'd care? "Naw, fuck it. But thanks for chasing him."

"No problem. Hey, let me get you guys shots. Be back."

"What do you want to do?" My girl asks.

"I don't know."

"You ok?" She kisses my cheek. So soft. The music dimming. I think the last song of the night I heard was "World in My Eyes" by Depeche Mode. The crowd is dissipating into a haze.

"Yeah, I'm ok." I nuzzle her face, her ear, her hair. *Inhale her*.

She reaches a hand under the table and places it on my cock. "You want to go back to your hotel?"

"Yes," I say.

And we did.

Paris Coronavirus!

I remember it was a bitch to get out of Germany for some fucked up reason. End October/Early November 2019. I was in Berlin suffering with the gout and I was stuck in my hotel room for the weekend (in a snazzy joint down the street from 'Checkpoint Charlie') after I had been in Berlin 17 days and it was time to ramble but couldn't because of the gout and I desperately wanted to hit Belgium because I had never been and because I wanted to get out there before the snows came but there were no direct trains available, and so I said, ok, fuck it, we'll go to Cologne, instead; then, after we'll take the 90-minute train over the border but I couldn't do that either. All the trains were booked, flight costs were astronomical, *goddammit*. Ok, fine, I'll train-it up to Hamburg (had never been, glad I did), hang out a few days there, then, the train to Cologne, stay couple days (had been for World Cup 2006) *then*, the train to Brussels & Bruges. Simple, right?

Right.

Of course this was all pre-Coronavirus plague. Imagine doing that now? The absolute freedom to go and do whatever the fuck you wanted without worrying about a goddamn thing, least of all sitting on a train next to a stranger without a mask.

Now that I think about it, where this Covid misery started, not in China, *for me*, but in Paris. *A close-up view of the Corona*, as a matter of fact…

Early December 2019. That's when I first noticed the news on *DW, BBC. France 24*. Long before American TV bothered. Just *peeks* and *beeps* and *zonks* and *blips* about a new form of flu. Nothing major. After all, we were dealing with the national unions strike in Paris at the time, we had other things to worry about; I mean, *fuck,* we were watching as Paris burned, literally, during the protests. I wonder if that helped cause the initial spread there, 'super-spreader' events, you know? Hundreds of thousands took to the streets every day but even more so for the larger demonstrations that took place on Saturdays along with an equal amount of cops. Imagine how many arrested and stuck in jail cells. How many injured and sardined into ERs? During the week personal automobile traffic in spots was jammed for twelve-fucking-hours daily. You couldn't get anywhere by vehicle until after 10pm. Metros, buses, trains, planes and roads were out. Streets overflowed with disheveled humanity. Restaurants and shops were packed with workers waiting for the traffic to subside. Shoulder to shoulder in outdoor cafes under wind-protectant-see-through tarps and heater lamps. Some customers had to crawl *on* others to get to the toilet. Hop one back of the chair to the next. Taking strangers hands to help you over.

You could sometimes smell the smoke from the fires the protestors set. Cars ablaze, motorbikes, taxis, buses, abandoned hotels, shop fronts, public toilets, and at the train stations they swarmed. Either by the protestors themselves or the people fighting, hand over fist, to get that ONE fucking train per hour (instead of the usual 6 or 7 rains per hour to get to work). All schools had closed. Hospitals. Museums. State services. Underground malls were ransacked by the protestors and beat any innocent passersby they came across. I missed that by a few minutes one day after I came out of an afternoon film at *Les Halles* near the Louvre.

Police countered with water cannons, horses, dogs, tear gas, armored vehicles. It's quite a sight to see walls of men sent rolling by the blasts of military-counter-terrorists water cannons and crashing into metal barriers and toppled over fences and public fountains and tumbling over statuary and benches and other people. Watching the nightly news broadcasts they'd report the movements of the rioters and you could hear them approaching your area, hear the helicopters, the bullhorns, the screams, smell the fires, the traffic suddenly coming to a halt right outside your window as armed police chased and beat back the crowds, and sometimes the crowds chased the police. *Absolute madness.* Nerve-fucking-wracking to say the least. Mom & Pop shops went under due to lack of business. Other seniors washed their hands of it all after lifetimes in the city and moved back to the countryside. Young families drove to neighboring countries to wait it out. Shelves began to empty in your neighborhood market because the goddamn deliveries weren't being made. Everything is controlled by the unions there. Of course, later, as the strike dragged into weeks wives forced their husbands out the door to become scab drivers and soon began driving trucks and making clandestine deliveries in the dead of night. I know. I saw them. People saw. Nodded their heads. However nobody, that I heard of, had reported them to the unions. Why? They were putting bread and eggs back into our lives. It's a scary feeling when you go to the produce section at your local and the displays are empty save for a few rotten throw-backs. You then have to sniff out other shops that may have fresher goods. Who managed to get a delivery of this or that? Simply put, after a month or so the shit was running out. And people panicked.

And so in this, I wonder if the illness I had suffered through around that same stretch was Corona-related, an earlier strain of the Covid. Indeed, French doctors confirmed in 2020 that the Corona began in Paris around November 2019. I find this out later, of course. At the time, I'll be honest, it got rotten-bad for me, kids. *I thought I was gonna die!*

Undetected? Under-reported? Ignored on purpose?

That's certainly what happened in Trump's case, he knew how bad it was January 2020 but chose to blow it off, he freely admitted so on tape to Bob Woodward… didn't want the market or people to panic, apparently not giving a good goddamn about the would be 500,000 Americans-thus far-that he helped cull from my country.

You noticed on the streets little by little. People sneezing around you. Dry coughing. Spitting. You felt like you were walking in a petri dish of flu-germs as you made your way down the road (same way you feel when you walk through the heart of the Tenderloin District in San Francisco. *The Zombies of Death*. Or, in my case, actually *stay* in a hotel in the middle of that cesspool for a week). Yes, one might reason, it could have been the cold weather, but these *Parisians* are a hearty breed, they're used to that winter climate. They know how to dress, what to expect.

Then it was in the cafes. Where I was living every day. Wake up late. An afternoon riser. *Why get up early?* I was crawling home from the bars in the morning…Grab my heavy coat (a los angeles warehouse wholesaler), my scarf (Irish imports shop Bayeux, Normandy), my gloves (thrift shop off the Republique, Paris), knit cap (same), and my cheap "book" bag, black, I got from the "The D" hotel in Downtown Las Vegas. It was a give-away toiletry bag from the casino that fit my laptop, notepad, pens, and chargers perfectly. With an over the shoulder carrying strap. I looked like a "professional" with that thing, better than hauling around a backpack. A man in his 40s, or a man of *any* age, should not be carrying monster-sized-overstuffed-backpacks into cafes, clubs, or bars. You look like a fuckin' child. And a douchebag. *And you get in the motherfucking way!*

Anyway…

The regulars I'd notice when I was in the cafes for dinner, to write, to chill before hitting the bars, began disappearing. Servers too. You'd ask the manager what happened to so-and-so.

Oh, Monsieur Jim, he is very sick, he is in hospital.

Or: *Poor Marianne, her brother says she is bed all week, no work for her. So sudden!*

And then it was the bosses . Their wives or other family members would stand in for them.

Woke up with a high fever.

Woke up with a bad cough.

Woke up not breathing right. It was terrible! We had to call the ambulance. And there were many people at hospital with the same thing!

What?! Jesus?!

Living in Paris I wanted to spend time in different parts of the city. North. South. Left Bank. Right. The best was *the left*, of course, where I eventually settled. But it was up in *Le Marais* (3rd/4th *arrondissement*), an outstanding neighborhood, that I'd wake up sniffling in the mornings. *Loads of snot*. Ok, it's freezing fucking cold, not used to it coming from Los Angeles, so it's expected. Next morning a tickle in the throat. Dry coughing. Drinking liters of water. Pound the aspirins, "Cutie"-oranges, hot shower. *Fight it off*. Much better later in the day. And then at night still going out, in the rain, the deepening cold, taking an *Uber* down to *Rue Rivoli* at the bottom of the hill, kinda-near the *Hotel de Ville*, where I'd visit *L'Art Brut Bistrot* in the alley, after midnight, to get huge fucking plates of fresh, cold sausage and the softest bread, best I had in Paris, and drink with "Nico", the owner, until way past closing, or *Uber* across the river to *Harry's Bar* and the jazz club next door. Same drinking privileges for me at the Jazz club. The kids in Paris *love* their Uncle Jim!

Come to think of it, the bars didn't seem to have *any* problems with stock during the strike. *Hmmm.* Interesting…The bars then kindof became a refuge from the barrage of strike news. For those of us who haunted the nights of Paris only had need for the booze, the women, the bars, the music, and the dark…there were always taxis or *ubers* if need be after 4am, when the streets were empty and silent and cold and only the lonely wandered…

I was in *Le Marais* for 12 days, but because of the strike my hotel was hit with 90% cancellations and had to close. People were afraid of the protests and violence (of which, as mentioned, there was an especially frightening fuck-load *after* dark, when the alcohol started to pour heavy for the young men who can't handle their shit) but mostly people couldn't *get into* the city. Roads were blocked by delivery trucks and buses.

I found a crap room down near the dreaded tourists' enclave off the corner of *Place Saint Michel* and *Rue Saint Germain.* Yes, there were fewer tourists all of a sudden, those who did make it were from Belgium or Germany or Holland, a handful of resourceful Americans, but still, fuckin' *tourists*. Mewling, pushing, crowding, loud, fluttering about aimlessly, flailing underfoot, getting on my nerves. *I was down the street from a McDonald's and a Chipotle for fuck's sake!* Though pleasantly also across the street from an independent cinema. Where I saw "The Lighthouse" (great film: the jerking-off & cum scene were especially harrowing; incredible work from Dafoe & Pattinson) clearing my throat, sniffling, and spitting into a napkin. Probably disturbing the handful of other middle-aged drunks who go to a 7:50pm show on a Wednesday night to get out of the cold, sleep off a happy-hour before dragging their asses back home to a crap life, or to jack-off as well.

Then, one night, in this tiny room in tourists' purgatory, I started a slight fever. I woke up sweating in bed. *What the fuck?* It would come on, the fever, I'd shiver violently, then, it would recede, like an outgoing wave, and I'd feel fine again. After a few nights of this, I began, only in bed, mind you, to develop a horrendous cough, worse in my life. *Choking.*

Belching. Farting. Body-Wracking. Face turning red. Head nearly popping off. That would calm down and then I'd get dreadful bouts of shortness-of-breath. I had to fight to keep my spirit from escaping. I thought somebody was sitting on me. I pounded on my chest with my fist to get the breathing going again. *What the fuck was happening?* Then, I'd pass out the rest of the night.

I had energy during the day. I wasn't light-headed, wasn't sneezing. I went about shopping, getting in my daily coffee and writing sessions at a decent café I found in the area. I went to cinema further down *Saint Germain* where they have a cluster of them and two cozy bars for after-movie drinking. The Mulled wine was a great treat after the movies…

Only twice more I woke up in a sweat though the outside temp was in the mid-20s. And then I began spitting up *gobs* of ridiculous phlegm overnight. *I'd hock out large splotches of ruby red blood too with that phlegm. CHRIST!* Never felt so sick in my life. I heard the death rattle. I was done for. *Scared the fuck out of me!*

But being Latino, naturally-stubborn, afraid of doctors and their dire news and warnings and the fact I had spent the last 7 years of my mother's life in and out of hospitals made me all the more suspect of such places and thus, stupidly, I did not seek the assistance of a house-call doctor nor did I think about going to an ER. I was in *Paris* goddammit. *I wasn't going to die here!* Fuck that. I'll take care of this on my own.

This went on for 30 days.

When we were younger, a thousand years ago, and got sick, we clung to the age-old Mexican *treatment* of "drink a 7up…eat saltines…take an aspirin"…..well, not this time (though, oddly enough, that shit *does* work for some things).

I sought out alternative/natural pharmacies after the usual suspects of name-brand cough syrups, gooey-green liquids loaded with enough alcohol to knock out a bull, and various powdered vitamin-boosts didn't work.

Vicks VapoRub (tried & true throwback to Mom's remedies), "natural" cough drops (no, not *Ricola*, something French) and bottles of a syrupy concoction recommended by the pharmacist off *Rue Ecoloes* made up of chamomile, roots of god knows what, saffron, other flowers and ginger and the fuck else if I know, the ingredients label was in French. (Photo of that bottle on my Instagram, January 6th, 2020 @thebeastlywriter) Finished one bottle and half of a second.

And, day by day, inch by motherfuckin' inch, I got better. But first, bouts of crying were the order of the night. And wicked, forked tongued cursing. And wishing you *were* dead. No sleep. Anxious thoughts of how they'd find your bloated and blue body face-down on the floor, collapsed, on the way to the toilet. Bowels voided. Underwear and ass and crotch soiled. Vomit and shit and piss puddled on the carpet beneath you. *An unholy stench!* Having died alone and nobody knew nor cared.

You can get a reading of how well you're doing by how many wads of tissue you see scattered around your bed after a rough night: entire boxes spent, wadded up with blood. Then, down to half a box. Then, down to a few snowballs scattered near the wastebasket. *Until one day you wake up and the floor is clean enough to eat off of!* And I could walk *without* shortness of breath. And drink to the wee hours again. *Hallelujah!* Never prayed so much in my damn life. Except when Mom was dying in the hospital for three weeks and I'd go to the chapel *before* and *after* I visited her and prayed so fucking hard I nearly had a heart attack.

I remained in Paris without so much as an itch on my considerable ass. I toured, hit bookshops, cinemas, drank in bars til 7am-8am-9am, bedded French girls, *wrote a book at a café in Hemingway's old neighborhood*, and just *lived*, motherfucker! *I was so happy.* So relieved. I beat whatever the hell *that* was. The national strike had finally come to an unofficial end, the asshole in the WH brought us to the brink of war with Iran, and I didn't want to leave.

I wasted time with being sick and the strike. I wanted to make up for it. I tried to hang on as long as possible but the cash was running low, it was getting colder by the minute, this super-flu seemed to be popping up everywhere, and soon the French government was encouraging people to return to their home countries (wish I hadn't: only to come back for the lock-downs with an ineffectual and incompetent sociopath to lead us astray and into the mouth of madness).

Alas, in February, I made my escape. Smartly flew out of Orly. Grabbed an hour's flight to Dublin. Spent 10 days in the heart of the Temple Bar District where it was brutally cold and snowing; a storm had battered Ireland, and I walked in that snow and wind but mostly rain for days on-end hitting their pubs.

Because I had trekked across Ireland 20 years previous and had seen the touristy side of it already, all I did was chill this time. Drank, hung out with the locals, attended Martin McDonagh's new play *The Lieutenant of Inishmore* at the 'Gaiety Theatre' (good shit), went to the Savoy Cinema to catch "Birds of Prey" (first hour sucked, second great action, but overall tone mangled), chatted up the boys & girls behind the stick where I was graciously invited to join in on the after-hour "lock-ins" every night, and ate well. It was glorious. Sickness a distant memory.

After, I flew 9.5 hours from Dublin to San Francisco. First time on American soil in 7 months. I fucking LOVE 'Frisco'. One of the most

European-American cities there is. Plenty of cafes, bars-*hell, a bar every two fucking feet*-proper public transport, *the bay*, tons of Euros mucking about, independent coffeeshops, cozy neighborhoods, and on the second day I started to *heave*-cough again. *Goddammit!*

And spit phlegm. But clear this time. *No blood.* Then the shortness of breath returned. *Dammit.* Not again! Then, *poof,* it went away! *What the hell?*! My voice would also get hoarse after speaking a short while. *Bipolar symptoms to say the least!*

Two weeks later I reluctantly flew to Los Angeles, my birthplace. Checked into a Japanese hotel on the corner of Hill & 2nd Street in Downtown LA where I saw busloads of Chinese student-tourists pour into the lobby with gi-normous-fucking-trunks packed heavy and on rollers but still had to be dragged scraping across the floor, one in each hand. They were wearing masks & gloves.

Now, Paris has a huge Chinese community. They have their own "Chinatown", but Chinese New Year was cancelled and Chinatown was closed-off because of this new "superflu". And the sometimes-ready-topersecute-a-minority *(how the fuck do you think the nazis found the Jews so fast? they didn't exactly have GPS)* the French did not disappoint. When it came time to point fingers at the Chinese they did, and scold, and wrote appalling headlines in the daily papers *("Yellow Fever Comes to Paris!")* and once emptied an entire metro car when a young Chinese girl walked on and sat while wearing a mask and left her sobbing all the way home.

Some Asians wore T-shirts that read DON'T SPIT ON ME! I'M NOT CHINESE! I'M SOUTH KOREAN (or, Vietnamese, Japanese, etc).

Good God…

February 2020 back in L.A. (and coincidentally is when I'm coming out with this book, a year later).

Along with the cough. *Fuck!* Spit phlegm at night but again *no blood.* Got winded though while walking. *Motherfucker!* I thought it was the cluttered air of Downtown LA, radical climate conditions. *It was 90-fucking-degrees first day back!*

I hightailed it to Pasadena north of L.A. Open spaces, near the San Gabriel Mountains, the racetrack in Arcadia…dive bars…cheap food, that funky, laid-back-smoke-weed-vibe, it was magic. But the coughing fits reared up. *And what's with being short of breath again?* By this time Coronavirus was in full bloom, and seeing what was happening on the news-the quarantines, overcrowded hospitals, the death tolls updated every minute like the odds at a sportsbook in a Downtown Las Vegas casino-I decided I wasn't that bad off.

The coughing ceased though I hocked up clear phlegm in the mornings *for months*. The off & on shortness of breath *stayed until May of 2020!* After spending a frigid month in Manhattan Beach and then a month in the sweltering but dry heat of Las Vegas I began to eat and drink like a Beast again. Surprisingly, I haven't had my allergies, or any other common ailments since. Well, a few piercing headaches, pain that sears like an ice pick into my head then simply disappears in a second it takes to blink. I've dropped small items on occasion. I forget inconsequential details, takes me an extra beat to remember the name of a film or director.

Did I have the Corona before it went global? Perhaps it was a case of exaggerated pneumonia. Or maybe it's my heart finally giving out. I know I've been damn lucky, but at the same time what the fuck do I know?

The Coronavirus is still raging across the planet as of this writing, early 2021…lock-downs are here…LA became the nation's ground zero for a cup of coffee…Trump conducted a failed insurrection *on his own government* last month…The vaccine had a poor roll out thanks to the last administration…Joe Biden is our president now and it seems like maybe somebody finally gives a goddamn. And is thankfully COMPETENT….International travel is banned. Hell, flying up to Frisco will get you a 14-day quarantine, but why even bother because everything is still closed up like a bastard there, worse than L.A…

To be safe I pound multiple vitamins. Eat tons of fruit. Drink pots of green tea. Wash my hands a hundred times a day. *Wear my mask.* Social distance. I write. I read. I consume *Netflix. Amazon Prime.* Watch *CNN* religiously. I masturbate to memories of past loves and long ago, slippery conquests, and, of course, I continue to drink my 7up…eat my saltines…and take my aspirin.

Though I haven't been sick in 9 months, it continues to get worse all around me as I sit here in the heart of Koreatown, off Western & Wilshire. Sirens wail in the middle of the night. Incessant. Calling. Seeking. Vengeful. Whose father was that? Crosses my mind as I toss and turn. In my nightmares I can see an indiscriminate mist visiting door to door. Whose mother? Grandmother? Uncle? Child? Teacher. Cop. Doctor. Nurse. Artist. Security guard. Waitress. Writer. Grocery store clerk. Etc. Etc. Etc…

Last Word

Ok, that's it for now. Hope you liked it as much as I enjoyed writing it. Later this year, *have no fucking clue when*, be on the lookout for ***A Mexican-American in Paris: Beastly Tales Romping Across Pre-Covid Europe. The Writer's Cut! Vol. 2***.

We'll have pieces on…

Krakow, Poland:

Staying in a loft in the old Jewish Quarter, exploring their ancient, local bars, and two highly dramatic excursions: 1) Visiting ***Auschwitz & Birkenau***: it's taken me a while to process that day (we've been through a fucking pandemic since then, you know, other shit to worry about). And it *is* a full fucking day for the ride out there and the visiting of the two sites. You have to go in groups as part of a tour. *NO* single travelers allowed due to fear of lone wolf terrorist acts. Serious. 2) The afternoon at ***Oskar Schindler's Factory***. A site that now houses a permanent exhibit on the Nazi Occupation of Krakow. Honestly? I found that to be more terrifying. With tons of material available to examine it was *palpable*, off putting; videos, audio, photos, furniture, artifacts, vehicles, weapons, *hell*, actual swastika wallpaper and flooring preserved and *it shattered me*. Whereas at the camps most of it has been razed and you're told by the guide what used to be *here*, what they did *there*, but much is left to the imagination. Yes, you're at a crime scene, the murder of millions of innocents, an atrocity, an abomination has taken place exactly where you stand, but still…*Dachau*, outside Munich, I visited in 1998, was a nightmare that haunts me to this day. I get the shivers thinking about that place. I published a major piece on that, with photos, in an international magazine at the time called *Gadfly*. *Terezin*, an hour outside Prague, I went Spring 2000, was a trip. Anyway…

Warsaw, Poland: My last name is *Marquez*. But traced back 500 years and it's *Markowitz*. And my ancestors comes from Warsaw. So there's that. Also, the underground bars, some on the eastern side of the river where the only language spoken is Russian and the next major destination if you continue east by train is Moscow. That, combined with the monuments all over the city from World War II and you have one damn interesting city.

Octoberfest. Munich, Germany:

What turned out to be the last one held, October 2019, due to the goddamn Covid. 'Nuff said.

Vienna, Austria:

The masterworks of Gustav Klimt. Mozart in concert at the Vienna Opera House. A famous, if underwhelming, slice of chocolate cake. Drinking nightly by the side of the Danube River. A frantic search for my pants across the city on moving day; Vienna to Krakow, *by propeller plane!!!*

Paris, France:

Drinking & fighting in the *Pigalle*.

Writing, with coffee & wine at this one tiny spot I discovered and frequented on the *Mouffetard*, up the hill from *Rue Monge*: Hemingway's old neighborhood.

Brussels & Bruges, Belgium.

Home of the French Fry. The ultimate waffles. Bars aplenty. Deathly cold. One city was magic, the other was a shithole.

Love & Whiskey,
Jimmy The Pen (aka The Beast) Marquez
12:33am. February 11, 2021
Pasadena, Calif.

Me love you long time, but remember, as usual, kisses cost extra.

Until then, baby-doll…

Instagram:@thebeastlywriter
Twitter:@beastlywriter
Facebook: Jim Marquez-Writer

www.ingramcontent.com/pod-product-compliance
Ingram Content Group UK Ltd.
Pitfield, Milton Keynes, MK11 3LW, UK
UKHW020141250726
13967UKWH00002B/785